"THE OLDEST BOOK KNOWN TO HUMANITY"

"The Tarot has affected the thinking of many cultures and many ages. An understanding of its symbolic meanings gives us a unique opportunity to master a significant part of occult wisdom.

"But most of us are interested in divination, and a major part of this book is devoted to how one may read the cards in terms of the actual problems of living people.

"When the cards are laid out for a reading, they reveal to the trained reader answers to some of the important concerns of life. Out of some unknown power in the cards comes revelation after revelation, and we learn from the Tarot some of the things we need to know to better order our lives."

(Eden Gray, *The Tarot Revealed*)

Signet Supernatural

THE TAROT REVEALED

A Modern Guide to Reading the Tarot Cards

by
EDEN GRAY

Revised and Updated

A SIGNET BOOK

NEW AMERICAN LIBRARY

Copyright © 1960, 1988 by Eden Gray

SIGNET TRADEMARK REG. U.S. PAT. OFF. AND FOREIGN COUNTRIES
REGISTERED TRADEMARK—MARCA REGISTRADA
HECHO EN CHICAGO, U.S.A.

SIGNET, SIGNET CLASSIC, MENTOR, ONYX, PLUME, MERIDIAN
and NAL BOOKS are published by NAL PENGUIN INC.,
1633 Broadway, New York, New York 10019

First Printing, November, 1969

22 23 24 25 26 27 28 29 30

PRINTED IN THE UNITED STATES OF AMERICA

INTRODUCTION

The very word *Tarot* seems to strike a hidden chord—the love of mystery—in the hearts of many when they first look upon the strange and beautiful cards of the Tarot pack. Questions are asked immediately. Are they used to divine the future? What is their history? What is the meaning of the symbols that appear on each card? What have they meant—and what do they still mean—to the student of the occult?

The complex and sometimes obscure character of most of the books on the subject has acted as a barrier rather than a help to people who are attracted to these ancient cards and would like to understand and use them. In the course of teaching many classes on the Tarot, I was frequently made aware of the student's need for an easily understood book—with instructions that could be followed without confusion, and with a clear explanation of the meaning of the symbols that constantly recur in the cards.

I have therefore tried in this book to present the ancient lore of the Tarot in a form that the beginning student can utilize. I have carefully extracted the original, basic meanings of the cards from a number of authentic sources, stressing those symbols that have persisted beneath the many guises the Tarot has assumed throughout the centuries. I have tried to put the meanings of the symbols and the interpretation of the cards in simple language, so that the beginner can easily take the plunge and begin to use the cards in divination and contemplation.

Few have the leisure to make a profound study of an art like the Tarot; but there is much to be learned from even an introductory study of these historical, magical cards and their symbolism. It is my hope that people will find this book a convenient path into an endlessly exciting and rewarding realm.

—E. G.

CONTENTS

1.

THE MAGIC IS IN THE CARDS

The Tarot pack consists of 78 cards: 56 contained in four suits (the forerunners of modern playing cards), called THE MINOR ARCANA; and 22 additional picture cards, known as THE MAJOR ARCANA. The Major Arcana are said to be derived from the pages of the oldest book in the world, originated by Hermes Trismegistus, councillor of Osiris, King of Egypt, at a period when hieroglyphic writing, magic, astrology, and other mystic sciences flourished. Some scholars maintain that they were invented by the Chinese; others that they were brought from India by the Gypsies. They are also frequently related to the Kabalistic lore of the Hebrews; and a correspondence is often pointed out between the cards of the Major Arcana and the letters of the Hebrew alphabet.

Although the earliest known date (1390 AD) is attributed to a Tarot pack displayed in a European museum, it is almost certain that the history of the cards goes back even further into the shrouded mists of antiquity. One interesting story of their origin is that after Alexandria was destroyed, the city of Fez became the intellectual capital of the world, to which wise men traveled from far and wide. In order to communicate more easily—for they spoke in many tongues—they set about creating a universal language, which they embodied in a book of pictures abounding in mystic symbols. A key to the interpretation of these universal symbols and their infinite combinations, it is said, enabled the

11

sages to understand one another and to create a common store of wisdom. It is these pictures which are supposed to have come down to us in the form of the cards of the Major Arcana.

All of these accounts of the Tarot's origin add depth and interest to the cards, and none of them can be *denied*. A profound study of the Tarot does reveal much of the ancient Hebrew wisdom of the Kabala; many of the symbols are indeed linked with Egyptian mythology; and the Gypsies are widely considered to have possessed, from time immemorial, an uncanny gift for reading the past, the present and the future, by means of the Tarot pack.

It is entirely understandable that, in addition to the great body of authentic lore that has grown up around these remarkable cards, there is also a certain amount of myth, superstition and pure speculation about them. And, like a living language, they have undergone constant growth and change. As the messages contained in them were handed down through one group of initiates to another, many legends and mysteries were added to them. But underneath all the legends and the theories, it seems that some sort of indestructible, irreducible wisdom remains to reward and inspire the student; and sages and prophets throughout human history have uncovered in them secrets of universal meaning for man.

In recent times, too, many scholars and philosophers have been influenced by, or found inspiration in, "this oldest book known to man." Creative writers and psychologists have regarded the symbols and images of the Tarot with profound respect for their connection with the subconscious activities of the human mind. Among those who have dealt with it in various ways are: T. S. Eliot, in THE WASTE LAND; Charles Williams, in THE GREATER TRUMPS; William Lindsay Gresham, in NIGHTMARE ALLEY; and P. D. Ouspensky, in

A NEW MODEL OF THE UNIVERSE. The poet W. B. Yeats belonged to a secret order that dealt with the Tarot's occult traditions, while followers of the famous psychoanalyst, C. G. Jung, see in the Tarot cards symbols related to the archetypes of the collective unconscious. Albert Pike's MORALS AND THE DOGMA OF THE SCOTTISH RITES makes reference to the Tarot cards. Thomas Troward, one of the founders of New Thought and one of the clearest exponents of the Science of Mind, has devoted serious thought to the spiritual significance of these extraordinary pictures.

Thus it can be seen that the Tarot has affected the thinking of man in many cultures and many ages. An understanding of their symbolic meanings gives us a unique opportunity to master a significant part of occult wisdom. Symbols are the picture forms of inner thought; they have rightly been called the doors leading to the hidden chambers of the mind, and the study of them can be a fascinating pursuit in itself, conducive to contemplation and meditation.

But most of us are interested in divination, and a major part of the books about the Tarot (including this one) is devoted to how one may read the cards in terms of the actual problems of living people. When the cards are laid out for a reading (see Chapter IV), the way in which they fall and the relation of one card to the other reveal to the trained reader answers to some of the important concerns of life. They give us a method for interpreting character and throwing light on the future. They analyze the mind and spirit, often revealing unconscious motivations, hidden fears and anxieties that may be operating to hamper one's progress. Many clues that arise from the subconscious mind can be glimpsed in the reading. If one is functioning on a too material plane, the signs will be in the cards; if on a spiritual plane, this will be made

13

manifest, too. There are indeed treasures here for those seeking wisdom and guidance. Out of some unknown power in the cards, comes revelation after revelation, and we learn from the Tarot some of the things we need to know to better order our lives.

Here I should like to refer to the many systems of thought that have been superimposed on the Tarot at various times in history in the attempt to penetrate its meaning. The cards have been explained by philosophies and techniques based on Rosicrucian thinking, Numerology, Astrology, the signs of the Zodiac, the Hebrew alphabet, Color Symbolism and others. Whether one or another of these systems were used, the cards and their infinite combinations seemed to retain their powers of revelation. For myself, I have chosen to go back, as far as possible, to the original meaning of the pictures—without concentrating on any of the methods mentioned, but with respect for the contributions made by all of these schools of thought. Indeed it may be that the deepest occult wisdom of the Tarot cannot be put into words at all; only some of the distilled essence can be transmitted and, in the end, the seeker is told only what he cannot find for himself.

I'd like to add a general word here as to how one goes about reading the cards. In the techniques described in this book, the subject of the reading shuffles the cards, concentrating on a question he would like to have answered. The question itself may serve merely as a starting point; actually, it may represent only a small part of what will subsequently be revealed. The reader lays out the cards in the manner prescribed, and the way in which the cards fall tells the story, in accordance with the divination meanings which the reader has mastered.

In order to embark on your study, you will need a good deck of Tarot cards. Those pictured in this book belong to the Rider pack of E. A. Waite.

There are, of course, other versions of the pack, but the author recommends the use of the Rider pack, particularly in connection with the study of this book, since she has found the pictures in this pack the clearest and the best delineated.

But until you have learned the *meanings* of the pictures, don't take the readings you get too seriously. Obviously, it would be a mistake to act upon conclusions derived from fragmentary knowledge. In reading the cards, I would suggest that interpretations of the present—and, even more, those dealing with the future—should be of a positive, healing and helpful nature. No one should undertake to read his own cards, except as an exercise in layout and purely as an experiment. A far more objective reading, uninfluenced by one's own wishful thinking or undue fears, will be derived from a reading by another student.

Anyone, with a certain amount of application, can learn to read the cards with skill. But one who has more than the usual psychic and psychological insight can bring to the reading a broader, deeper, more subtle understanding. THE MAGIC IS IN THE CARDS—what one accomplishes with them will mirror the level of one's own development.

2.

THE MINOR ARCANA

The Minor Arcana consist of 56 cards equally divided into four suits comparable to the suits of our present-day playing cards:

		Associated with	Identified with
WANDS	=Clubs	Enterprise & Glory	Fire
CUPS	=Hearts	Love & Happiness	Water
SWORDS	=Spades	Strife & Misfortune	Air
PENTACLES	=Diamonds	Money & Interest	Earth

Each of the four suits comprises 14 cards, 10 numbered from Ace to Ten, and 4 Court cards—King, Queen, Knight and Page. In readings, the King often symbolizes *the Spirit;* the Queen, *the Soul;* the Knight, *the Ego;* and the Page, *the Body*.

Court cards sometimes represent situations rather than people in a reading. PAGES may represent either boys or girls. KNIGHTS often represent the coming or going of a matter.

The characteristics of the suits and Court cards given above are merely broad, general ones. In the pages immediately following, each of the cards is described, along with its divinatory meaning. When the pack is shuffled thoroughly, some of the cards naturally fall in an "upside-down" position; therefore the meaning of the "reversed" position is also given. Methods of laying out the cards for a reading are described in Chapter IV.

Readings depend not only on the way in which the cards fall in the layout, but on their nearness to, and combination with, other cards and the frequency with which cards of a given suit recur. For example, if you find many Wands in the layout, it will most likely indicate change; many Cups, good news and happiness; many Swords, striving; many Pentacles, wealth.

The Suits of the Minor Arcana

WANDS (Clubs)
This suit indicates animation and enterprise, energy and growth. The wands shown in the cards are always in leaf, suggesting the constant renewal of life. Their position in relation to other cards in the layout will determine whether the energy will be constructive or turned to opposition and quarreling. Cards in this suit are often associated with the world of ideas, and with creation or agriculture.

CUPS (Hearts)
This suit generally indicates love and happiness. The sign of the cup, which appears in all the cards of this suit, refers to water—a symbol of love, instruction, pleasure, knowledge. These cards usually express the good life, fertility, beauty—the emotions rather than the intellect.

SWORDS (Spades)
Swords generally represent the quest, aggression, ambition, boldness, force, courage. But they can

sometimes also mean transformation, hatred, war, if associated with certain other cards. They represent the world of activities—both constructive and destructive.

PENTACLES (Diamonds)
The symbols shown on the cards of this suit are pentacles, coins, consisting of circles surrounding 5-pointed stars made of intersecting triangles. They generally point to matters connected with money, material gain, attainment on the financial plane. They may also refer to development, trade, industry.

In medieval times the pentacles were seals or metal discs inscribed with various magic formulae. In the suit of Pentacles they are inscribed with pentagrams, the five-pointed star. This figure is the time-honored symbol of the magical arts and also the five senses of man, the five elements of nature and the five extremities of the human body.

THE WANDS

THE ACE OF WANDS

DESCRIPTION: A hand comes out from a cloud holding a flowering wand. In the distance is a mountain peak surmounted by a castle.

DIVINATORY MEANING: The beginning of an enterprise, creation or invention. A birth, the starting of a family or of a fortune, possibly an inheritance.

REVERSED: The new enterprise may not materialize. Clouded joy, false starts.

ACE of WANDS.

THE TWO OF WANDS

DESCRIPTION: A man of property looks out from his battlements over the sea; he holds a globe in his right hand and a staff in his left. Another staff is fixed in a ring. Roses and lilies are crossed on the left side of the card.

DIVINATORY MEANING: Lord of the manor. Riches, fortune, magnificence, dominion. Interest in scientific methods.

REVERSED: Physical suffering, sadness, domination by others.

THE THREE OF WANDS

DESCRIPTION: A calm, stately man, with his back turned, looks out to sea as his ships come into port. He has accomplished what the man in the Two of Wands was just beginning.

DIVINATORY MEANING: Trade, commerce, established strength, help from a successful merchant.

REVERSED: Beware of help offered. Wealth and position may slip away. Caution against pride and arrogance.

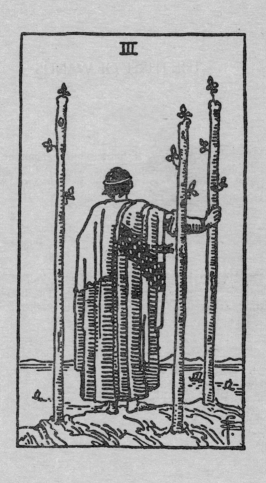

THE FOUR OF WANDS

DESCRIPTION: A garland is hung from the tops of four flowering wands; two maidens lift up bouquets of flowers; near them is a bridge over a moat, leading to an old castle.

DIVINATORY MEANING: The coming of romance, harmony, prosperity, peace. The bounty of the harvest home, perfected work, haven of refuge.

REVERSED: Here the meaning remains unaltered; it is still prosperity, increase and bounty, but in lesser degree.

THE FIVE OF WANDS

DESCRIPTION: A group of young men are shown brandishing wands as if in combat. It may be mimic warfare.

DIVINATORY MEANING: Strenuous competition, strife. Struggle in trying to attain riches and success. The battle of life. There may be quarreling and a lawsuit.

REVERSED: New business opportunties. A compromise is reached.

THE SIX OF WANDS

DESCRIPTION: A horseman wearing a laurel wreath of victory carries a wand which is also covered with a wreath. Footmen carrying wands accompany him.

DIVINATORY MEANING: Triumphal procession, victory after strife, gain. Good news and conquest, advancement in the arts and sciences.

REVERSED: Indefinite delay, fear of a victorious enemy.

THE SEVEN OF WANDS

DESCRIPTION: A young man on a rocky hill grasps a flowering wand. Six others rise up against him. In Queen Elizabeth I's time, men fought in this manner.

DIVINATORY MEANING: Man holding his own against adversaries. Strife, stiff competition in business, war or trade; success against opposition; courage in the face of difficulties.

REVERSED: Perplexity, embarrassment, anxiety. This card is also a caution against indecision.

THE EIGHT OF WANDS

DESCRIPTION: A flight of wands is shown passing through open country; they seem to be coming to the end of their course.

DIVINATORY MEANING: Haste, hope, movement in affairs. The arrows of love, messages, letters, journey by air.

REVERSED: Arrows of jealousy, quarrels, domestic disputes.

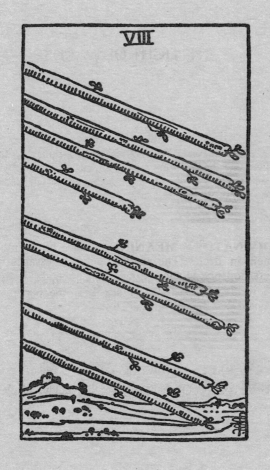

THE NINE OF WANDS

DESCRIPTION: A man, his head bound with a bandage, leans upon his staff, as if awaiting an enemy. Behind him stand eight wands in orderly procession like a palisade.

DIVINATORY MEANING: Preparedness, strength in reserve, opposition. If attacked, the person involved will defend himself stoutly.

REVERSED: Obstacles, adversity, delay, displeasure.

THE TEN OF WANDS

DESCRIPTION: A man carries a heavy burden consisting of ten flowering wands. He is bowed down by their weight as he plods toward the city.

DIVINATORY MEANING: One who is carrying an oppressive burden but will manage to reach his goal. Power unwisely used. Problem soon to be solved.

REVERSED: Treachery, duplicity, separation, emigration. If there is a lawsuit, it will probably be lost, unless one is vigilant.

THE PAGE OF WANDS

DESCRIPTION: Against a background of mounds or pyramids, a page makes a proclamation. He represents the eternal messenger.

DIVINATORY MEANING: Blond, blue-eyed young man, faithful lover, messenger, postman, bearer of tidings. He may represent a child, either boy or girl. If this card appears next to a card representing a man, there will be favorable testimony concerning him.

REVERSED: Unpleasant news, indecision about a project.

PAGE of WANDS.

THE KNIGHT OF WANDS

DESCRIPTION: A handsome young knight in armor gallops across the plain. His mantle is decorated with salamanders, symbolizing the Suit of Fire. The pyramids in the distance are symbols of the earth in its natural aspect and are also related to fire. They are seen again in the Page and Queen of Wands.

DIVINATORY MEANING: A fair-haired, blue-eyed young man capable of creating conflict or rivalry. The card may mean departure, absence, flight, change of residence.

REVERSED: Division, interruption, discord. If in marriage, may betoken frustration.

KNIGHT of WANDS.

QUEEN OF WANDS

DESCRIPTION: A crowned queen wearing royal robes holds a flowering wand in her right hand, that of authority. In her left hand is a sunflower, signifying her control over nature. The lions on the arms of her throne are fire symbols, and the black cat is a symbol of Venus in its sinister aspect. The three pyramids are seen again.

DIVINATORY MEANING: A blonde, blue-eyed woman, animated and magnetic. Generally she lives in the country, is home-loving and nature-loving. She is friendly, chaste, and honorable. If the card beside her is a man, she is very fond of him; if a woman, she is interested in her welfare. The card may mean success in undertakings and enterprises.

REVERSED: A virtuous but strict and economical woman. Opposition, jealousy, deceit, or infidelity are suggested.

QUEEN of WANDS.

THE KING OF WANDS

DESCRIPTION: A crowned king holds a flowering wand. His robe is richly embroidered with mystic symbols; the lion symbol appears on the back of his throne. Beneath his crown he wears what is known as a "cap of maintenance."

DIVINATORY MEANING: A blond, blue-eyed man of enterprise and authority. Generally he is married and the father of a family living in the country. He is honest and conscientious and can also be impassioned and noble. The card may also betoken unexpected heritage, good marriage.

REVERSED: A severe, unyielding man, strict in his judgments. Suggests the possibility of opposition or quarrel. May also suggest advice that should be followed.

KING of WANDS

THE CUPS

ACE OF CUPS

DESCRIPTION: A hand reaches out from a cloud holding a cup from which five streams of living water fall into the lake below—a symbol of the subconscious mind. A dove of peace holds a wafer marked with a cross as the dew of Spirit descends onto the water lilies, which are symbols, like the lotus, of eternal life. A reminder here, that when you keep your mind filled with the Spirit it will fill your material cup to overflowing.

DIVINATORY MEANING: Abundance in all things. Love, joy, fertility. Nourishment from spiritual sources.

REVERSED: Hesitancy to nurture love, instability. The good beginning is cut short. Materiality.

ACE of CUPS.

THE TWO OF CUPS

DESCRIPTION: As a young man and maiden pledge their troth, above their cups the Caduceus of Hermes rises. A lion's head appears between the wings.

DIVINATORY MEANING: The beginning of a love affair or a spiritual union. Cooperation, partnership, balance of ideals, and plans with a kindred soul. Harmony between the masculine and feminine halves of our own nature.

REVERSED: Misunderstandings, possibility of broken plans or engagement. Parting of the ways. Passion that is too violent.

THE THREE OF CUPS

DESCRIPTION: Three maidens in flowing robes raise high their cups in a place of flowering fruits and foliage. They are pledging friendship.

DIVINATORY MEANING: Conclusion of a matter in plenty, perfection and gayety. Happy issue, victory, liberality, abundance. A healing to come.

REVERSED: Excess of physical enjoyment and pleasure in the senses.

THE FOUR OF CUPS

DESCRIPTION: Seated under a tree, a young man contemplates three cups on the grass before him. Out of a cloud in the sky comes a hand offering him another cup. He is nevertheless discontented.

DIVINATORY MEANING: Discontent with environment, but hesitancy to embark on a new venture. Contemplation, dissatisfaction with material success, re-evaluation of one's earthly pleasures.

REVERSED: New instructions, new relationships, novelty.

THE FIVE OF CUPS

DESCRIPTION: A mysterious figure in a dark cloak looks at three fallen cups, while two others stand upright behind him. In the background, a bridge leads to a small castle.

DIVINATORY MEANING: Vain regret, loss, but with something left over. Inheritance, patrimony, but not up to one's expectations. Can mean marriage, but may carry with it bitterness and frustration. Rejection of pleasure.

REVERSED: Hopeful expectations, a new alliance, return of an old friend.

THE SIX OF CUPS

DESCRIPTION: In a village green a boy offers a girl a cup of flowers. The manor house in the background suggests home and happy childhood memories. The other five flower-filled cups suggest beauty and abundance.

DIVINATORY MEANING: A card of the past and memories. Looking back on childhood things that have vanished. It may be the beginning of new relationships, new knowledge, new environment, or a meeting.

REVERSED: Living in the past, clinging to outworn symbols and associations. Possibility of an inheritance, or a gift from the past.

THE SEVEN OF CUPS

DESCRIPTION: Fantastic visions rise out of the cups—wreaths, jewels, snakes and towers—all resting on clouds. A man garbed in black contemplates the strange prodigies.

DIVINATORY MEANING: The seeker has had too many different ideas and desires, all in the realm of the imagination; great dreams; castles in the air. Some attainment but nothing substantial as yet. His forces have been scattered.

REVERSED: Good use of determination and will; a project about to be realized.

THE EIGHT OF CUPS

DESCRIPTION: A man with a staff walks away from the cups of his previous happiness. Streams, mountains and rocks lie before him. The moon turns an inscrutable face on him.

DIVINATORY MEANING: The rejection and decline of an undertaking; abandoning the present situation; the matter may be of slight consequence for good or evil. May indicate disappointment in love. The subject may desire to leave material success for something higher.

REVERSED: Joy, feasting, merriment. The spiritual aspect is abandoned for the material.

THE NINE OF CUPS

DESCRIPTION: This is the wish card. If it comes up in a spread, a wish may be made. The picture here is of a well-fed, well-satisfied man, perhaps a rich merchant (or woman of property) who has arranged his wealth in an ordered fashion.

DIVINATORY MEANING: Material success, assured future, physical satisfaction for the subject of the reading. Victory, well-being, robust physical health.

REVERSED: Mistakes, imperfections in present plans, overindulgence in food and drink.

IX

THE TEN OF CUPS

DESCRIPTION: Ten cups are shown in a rainbow. A man and woman below, evidently husband and wife, look upon the vision in wonder and worship. Two children are dancing near them.

DIVINATORY MEANING: Happy family life, true friendship, lasting success, happiness to come. Attainment of the heart's desires.

REVERSED: Loss of friendship, betrayal, chances of a family quarrel.

THE PAGE OF CUPS

DESCRIPTION: A handsome young man is shown as he contemplates a fish rising from the cup. The fish symbolizes pictures in the imagination taking form. In the background is the sea.

DIVINATORY MEANING: A young man or girl with light brown hair and hazel eyes. Studious, thoughtful, with an active imagination. Willing to render service to the seeker. Can mean news, a message, the birth of a child; in business, new methods proposed.

REVERSED: Obstacles, deception may soon be uncovered. Water in some form always indicates the subconscious mind. Here it is also the creator of new ideas and plans concerning love in one of its many aspects.

PAGE of CUPS.

THE KNIGHT OF CUPS

DESCRIPTION: A knight riding quietly and wearing a winged helmet, symbol of imagination. He is contemplative, not warlike; he bears his cup firmly as the horse prepares to cross the stream and approach the distant peaks.

DIVINATORY MEANING: A young man with light brown hair and hazel eyes, of high intelligence and romantic dreams. Love may come from him to the subject of the reading. He may also be the bearer of messages. May indicate advances, a proposition or an invitation.

REVERSED: Propositions should be carefully looked into. There may be subtlety, fraud, trickery, rivalry.

KNIGHT of CUPS.

THE QUEEN OF CUPS

DESCRIPTION: A queen sits on her throne contemplating an ornate, closed cup, signifying that what it contains of dreams and desires is not to be told abroad. Her throne is surrounded by the waters of the subconscious and is decorated with ondines (water nymphs).

DIVINATORY MEANING: This is a woman with light brown hair and hazel eyes. She is the beloved, the good wife and mother. She has the gift of vision, is poetic and imaginative. She dreams, but also acts out her dreams. Love, happy marriage, vision.

REVERSED: May be a good woman in some ways but is sometimes perverse. May indicate dishonesty, immorality.

QUEEN of CUPS.

THE KING OF CUPS

DESCRIPTION: A king is shown with a sceptre in his left hand and a large cup in his right. His throne rests upon the sea; a ship is seen at one side and a dolphin rises at the other. (Note that water, the symbol for the subconscious, appears in many of the Court cards.)

DIVINATORY MEANING: This represents a man with light brown hair and hazel eyes. He is a man of business, law, or divinity. He may be a bachelor. Friendly, of creative intelligence in the arts and sciences. He is disposed in favor of the subject of the reading. Kindness, liberality, generosity.

REVERSED: Man of violent, artistic temperament; could be dishonest, double-dealing. Can indicate considerable loss, scandal, injustice.

KING of CUPS.

THE SWORDS

THE ACE OF SWORDS

DESCRIPTION: Again we see a hand issuing from a cloud, this one grasping a sword, the point of which is encircled by a crown. Olive and laurel branches hang from the crown. Tongues of flame signify the descent of the spirit.

DIVINATORY MEANING: Great force in love as well as in hatred; excessive degree in everything; conquest and activity; triumph of power. May also mean fertility.

REVERSED: Too much power may lead to obstacles, disaster, tyranny.

ACE of SWORDS.

THE TWO OF SWORDS

DESCRIPTION: A blindfolded woman balances two swords upon her shoulders. She sits on a bench with her back to the sea. The crescent moon looks down upon her.

DIVINATORY MEANING: Balanced forces, stalemate, indecision, impotence, a temporary truce in family quarrels.

REVERSED: Release, movement of affairs, sometimes in the wrong direction. Caution against dealings with rogues.

THE THREE OF SWORDS

DESCRIPTION: A heart pierced by three swords. Rain and clouds in the background. A depiction of stormy weather.

DIVINATORY MEANING: Sorrow, tears, separation, delay. For a woman, the possible flight of her lover.

REVERSED: A meeting with one whom the subject has compromised. Disorder, confusion. Care should be taken against possible loss.

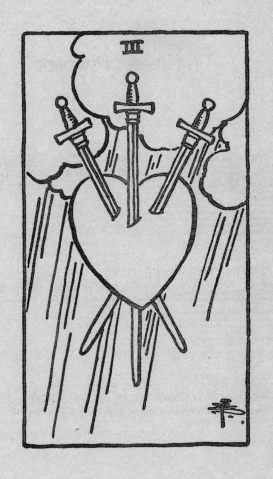

THE FOUR OF SWORDS

DESCRIPTION: The effigy of a knight lies at full length upon his tomb, in an attitude of prayer. One sword lies beside his tomb, while three hang over him.

DIVINATORY MEANING: Rest from strife; retreat; solitude. Hermit's repose; convalescence after illness; exile. Not a card of death.

REVERSED: Activity, social unrest, qualified success. Use precaution, economy and circumspection.

THE FIVE OF SWORDS

DESCRIPTION: A man looks scornfully at two dejected figures, whose swords lie upon the ground. He carries two swords on his left shoulder, and a third sword, in his right hand, points to the earth. Storm clouds fill the sky.

DIVINATORY MEANING: Conquest over others through physical strength. May betoken a threat to the subject of the reading.

REVERSED: Weakness, chance of loss and defeat. Stormy weather ahead.

THE SIX OF SWORDS

DESCRIPTION: A ferryman carries passengers in his boat to the opposite shore. The waters are smooth; the swords do not seem to weigh the boat down.

DIVINATORY MEANING: Passage away from difficulties; journey by water; success after anxiety; sending someone to represent you in an undertaking.

REVERSED: Unfavorable issue of an affair. No immediate way out of present difficulties. A stalemate.

THE SEVEN OF SWORDS

DESCRIPTION: A man is shown escaping with five swords, with two still remaining stuck in the ground. A nearby military camp is depicted.

DIVINATORY MEANING: Unstable effort, partial success. Uncertainty; a plan that may fail. The seeker finds someone trying to make away with that which is not his.

REVERSED: Good advice, counsel, instruction.

THE EIGHT OF SWORDS

DESCRIPTION: A bound woman standing in a watery waste is surrounded by swords. She is blindfolded. Behind her on a high crag stands a castle.

DIVINATORY MEANING: The seeker does not know which way to move in a situation. Bondage, crises, waste of energy in trivial detail, censure.

REVERSED: Freedom, relaxation from fear. New beginnings now possible.

THE NINE OF SWORDS

DESCRIPTION: A woman sits grieving on her couch while nine swords hang over her. This is the very depth of sorrow.

DIVINATORY MEANING: Inability to make a choice in an important matter. Doubt and desolation, failure, delay, misery, suffering. May mean death of a loved one.

REVERSED: Imprisonment, suspicion, doubt, shame.

THE TEN OF SWORDS

DESCRIPTION: Notice that in the other cards of this suit the swords merely surround the person, while here they actually pierce him. It is a scene of desolation, sorrow, and defeat. Tens of each suit are always the epitomes of the suits' meaning.

DIVINATORY MEANING: Misfortune, burdens to bear. May mean ruin, pain, utter defeat. Perhaps the death of a loved one.

REVERSED: Advantage, profit, power—but none of these are permanent. Courage to rise again, overthrow of adverse forces. In spiritual matters the suggestion is to look to a higher power for help.

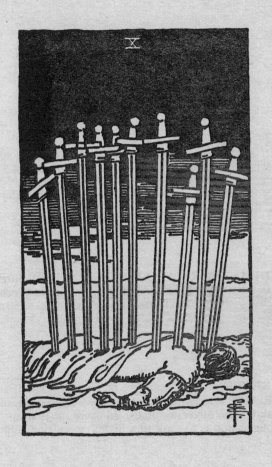

THE PAGE OF SWORDS

DESCRIPTION: A lithe young figure—either young man or maiden—holds a sword in both hands while walking over rugged land. Wild clouds are gathered about him. He looks around as if expecting an enemy.

DIVINATORY MEANING: An active, dark-haired, brown-eyed boy or girl. Betokens vigilance, scrutiny, spying for either good or evil.

REVERSED: Unprepared state; unforeseen events; may possibly mean illness; imposter likely to be defeated.

PAGE of SWORDS.

THE KNIGHT OF SWORDS

DESCRIPTION: A knight rides recklessly, at full speed, scattering his enemies. He symbolizes Galahad, the typical hero of romantic chivalry.

DIVINATORY MEANING: A dark-haired, brown-eyed young man strong and domineering, typifying skill and bravery. Someone about to rush headlong into the life of the seeker. The card may stand for skill, bravery, defense or war, conflict, and destruction. The cards on either side of this one in the layout should give an indication of the good or destructive influence to come.

REVERSED: Incapacity, extravagance, braggadocio.

KNIGHT of SWORDS.

THE QUEEN OF SWORDS

DESCRIPTION: A queen seated on a throne looks out over a cloud-filled landscape. Her right hand raises a sword whose hilt rests on the arm of her throne. She looks sorrowful and grave. (Note the storm clouds in all the Court cards of the Swords.)

DIVINATORY MEANING: A dark-haired, brown-eyed woman, subtle, keen and quick-witted. May signify widowhood, sterility, privation, separation, acquaintance with sadness. The sword of spirit penetrating matter and informing it.

REVERSED: A woman of artifice, prudery. May betoken narrow-mindedness, intolerance, bigotry.

QUEEN of SWORDS.

THE KING OF SWORDS

DESCRIPTION: A stern king, his sword un-sheathed, sits in judgment. Behind him on a banner are the butterflies of soul. They are also found on the queen's throne. The cypress trees of Venus stand out against a stormy sky.

DIVINATORY MEANING: A man with dark brown hair and brown eyes, he has the power of life and death. It may betoken a wise man, a counselor full of helpful ideas; whatever rises from authority, military, and government concerns, law, judgment.

REVERSED: A man who can be cruel, barbarous, unjust. Caution in matters that may result in a ruinous lawsuit.

KING of SWORDS.

THE PENTACLES

THE ACE OF PENTACLES

DESCRIPTION: The familiar symbol of a hand issuing forth from a cloud here holds the pentacle, while lilies grow in the garden below.

DIVINATORY MEANING: Perfect attainment. Ecstacy, felicity, bliss. Gold, prosperity, wealth.

REVERSED: Corruption of character by surplus wealth; the evil side of riches.

ACE of PENTACLES.

THE TWO OF PENTACLES

DESCRIPTION: A young man is dancing, with a pentacle in either hand. The pentacles are joined by an endless cord, which is like the number eight. Ships ride the high waves behind him.

DIVINATORY MEANING: Harmony in the midst of change; agility in handling situations. New projects are difficult to launch.

REVERSED: Simulated enjoyment and forced gayety. Inability to handle two situations at once that are in opposition. Messages in writing, letters of exchange.

THE THREE OF PENTACLES

DESCRIPTION: A sculptor is shown working in a monastery. This card should be compared with the Eight of Pentacles, where the worker was an apprentice. Here he has received his reward and is a mature artist.

DIVINATORY MEANING: Skill and mastery in trade, art and labor. Sometimes means nobility, aristocracy, renown and glory. Card of construction, material increase.

REVERSED: Mediocrity in workmanship, commonplace ideals, pettiness, weakness.

THE FOUR OF PENTACLES

DESCRIPTION: A crowned figure has a pentacle over his crown, two under his feet, while he clasps another with his hands and arms. He holds on firmly to what he has.

DIVINATORY MEANING: Clinging to material possessions. Love of earthly power. May indicate a miserly, ungenerous character. Possibility of inheritance, gifts, legacy.

REVERSED: Setbacks in material aspirations, chance of loss of earthly possessions. Obstacles, delay, opposition.

THE FIVE OF PENTACLES

DESCRIPTION: A destitute couple pass under a lighted window. The unfortunates in outer darkness have not yet realized the inner light. Note that the Fives of each suit are negative cards.

DIVINATORY MEANING: Material trouble, loneliness, destitution, spiritual impoverishment. Could mean unemployment, loss of home. Dark night of the soul.

REVERSED: Money regained, new employment, good companionship, new interest in business or spiritual matters.

THE SIX OF PENTACLES

DESCRIPTION: A merchant weighs money in the scales and distributes it to the needy. He shares his plentiful riches with others, out of the goodness of his heart and a sense of justice.

DIVINATORY MEANING: Philanthropy, charity, gifts. Alms dispensed with justice. Present prosperity shared with others.

REVERSED: Unfairness in business. Cause for envy, avarice, bad debt.

THE SEVEN OF PENTACLES

DESCRIPTION: A strong young farmer leans on his hoe as he watches his crops growing. Is he indolent or just contemplative?

DIVINATORY MEANING: Pause during the development of an enterprise. Possibly a stalemate with more energy needed before it can proceed. Growth or material possessions without effort.

REVERSED: Cause for anxiety over money. Little gain after much work. Unprofitable speculations.

THE EIGHT OF PENTACLES

DESCRIPTION: An artisan at his work, which he exhibits as trophies in the form of pentacles.

DIVINATORY MEANING: Apprenticeship. Skill in material affairs, craftsmanship, skill in both handiwork and business—sometimes merely in the preparatory stage. Employment or commission to come.

REVERSED: Voided ambition, unethical application of skill.

THE NINE OF PENTACLES

DESCRIPTION: A mature, well-dressed woman stands in her vineyard. There is a manor house in the background. The falcon on her wrist indicates her thoughts are as well controlled as the bird.

DIVINATORY MEANING: Material well-being, accomplishment, prudence, safety. There may be an inheritance from this woman or, if she seems to be the seeker, she will receive more wealth. Wisdom. A life well organized.

REVERSED: Roguery, dissipation, voided project, bad faith. Possible loss of home or friendship.

THE TEN OF PENTACLES

DESCRIPTION: A patriarch rests at ease in the foreground, surrounded by his family and dogs. An archway emblazoned with his coat of arms opens onto an impressive house.

DIVINATORY MEANING: An established family of material prosperity and lineage. Gain, riches, family matters, inheritance. May refer to money spent on a house or business property.

REVERSED: Chance of loss of inheritance. Family misfortune or loss of family honor. Robbery, gambling. Caution against getting involved in project that may be a poor risk.

THE PAGE OF PENTACLES

DESCRIPTION: The page is a youthful figure representing either a young man or maiden. He seems to be moving slowly, not seeing what is about him but staring fixedly at the pentacle in his raised hands.

DIVINATORY MEANING: A dark-haired, black-eyed boy or girl, careful and diligent. May be a bringer of messages. Reflection, scholarship, respect for learning, new opinions and ideas.

REVERSED: Dissipation, luxury, prodigality. The seeker is surrounded by those with ideas in opposition to his own. Unfavorable news.

PAGE of PENTACLES.

THE KNIGHT OF PENTACLES

DESCRIPTION: A knight rides a heavily caparisoned horse through a freshly plowed field. He balances the pentacle symbol carefully, as if he were displaying it but not really looking at it.

DIVINATORY MEANING: A black-haired, black-eyed young man, materialistic, methodical. Card betokens utility, serviceableness, patience, laborious toil, responsibility. May represent the coming or going of a matter.

REVERSED: Inertia, idleness, stagnation. A young man of careless habit.

KNIGHT of PENTACLES.

THE QUEEN OF PENTACLES

DESCRIPTION: A queen sits on her throne, which is covered with symbols of fruitfulness—cupids, goats, ripe fruit. A rabbit is in the foreground and a bower of roses is above her. She contemplates a pentacle which she holds in her lap.

DIVINATORY MEANING: A woman with black hair and black eyes. She is intelligent and thoughtful, a creator on the physical plane. She uses her talents well. Generosity, opulence, security, freedom from material lack.

REVERSED: Duties neglected, dependence on others. Suspicion, fear of failure and lack. Mistrust of those close to the seeker.

QUEEN of PENTACLES

THE KING OF PENTACLES

DESCRIPTION: A king sits on his throne, his robe emblazoned with many symbols of fruitfulness; his hand rests on the symbol of the pentacle. His castle appears in the background. The heads of bulls are shown behind him.

DIVINATORY MEANING: This is a black-haired, dark-eyed man, generally married. He may be a chief of industry. He is noted for his intelligence and character. Valor, reliability, mathematical gifts and success.

REVERSED: Perverse use of talents. Caution against association with gamblers and speculators.

KING of PENTACLES.

3.

THE MAJOR ARCANA

Far more significant than the cards of the Minor Arcana just described, are the twenty-two cards known as the Major Arcana—which cannot be associated with the modern playing-card deck. They are, in all probability, a concentrated version of Hermetic philosophy as later interpreted in the Kabala, Alchemy, Magic and Astrology. They comprise a psychological study of man in his relationship to the world of the spirit and to the physical world. Their symbolism is a type of shorthand for metaphysics and mysticism. Here are truths of so subtle and divine an order that to express them baldly in human language would be a sacrilege. Only esoteric symbolism can reveal them to the inner spirit of the seeker.

The Major Arcana are numbered from zero to twenty-one, each bearing a title which, to some degree, describes the card. Each card represents a distinct principle, law, power or element in Nature. The designs on the cards also illuminate the life of man, his joys and sorrows, hopes and despairs. They further indicate his search for the wisdom which enables him to control his passions and help in his transition to higher spheres, where he enters into the things of the spirit.

These picture-symbols are drawn from a deep store of images common to all men, everywhere, in all ages; images drawn from what has been called "the collective unconscious." They appear in our dreams, in the creative fantasies of poets, in the visions of saints and prophets. We *see* before we *say;* words are labels for man's visual imagination; thinking in pictures is a basic activity of the human mind. Many of the symbols in the Major Arcana—and especially those which are not specifically explained in the descriptions of the individual cards—are defined in the *Glossary of Symbols* at the end of the book.

With an understanding of the meaning of the cards of both the Minor and the Major Arcana, and the additional information given in the specimen readings and in the *Glossary of Symbols,* the student will be well on his way to understanding the great mysteries and wisdom of the ages. All knowledge and his own personal experience will be more easily understandable to him. Any book on the occult will be more readily comprehended. And any of these twenty-two cards of the Major Arcana can be the foundation for a great deal of meditation and inner enlightenment.

In addition to this, he will soon be convinced that there is some power present when the cards are read that directs their distribution. An extra-physical power (now demonstrated in our universities as "psychokinetic effect") cooperates with the unconscious muscular activities of the person using the deck and tends to affect the cards, as they are shuffled and cut, so that, when dealt, they fall into positions that have significance in relation to the subject to the reading.

THE FOOL, Card #0, can, in a sense, be compared to the Joker in the modern deck of cards—in that it has no assigned place in the deck, but stands more or less alone. Some writers on the Tarot, in

order to carry out their own interpretation, place
THE FOOL between the twentieth and the twenty-
first cards, but there is no concrete evidence that
this card belongs in that position or, for that matter,
as the first card of the Major Arcana. Rather, this
is a separate card—a third part of the deck—the
sum total of all.

THE KEYS

KEY 0—THE FOOL

DESCRIPTION: The Fool is depicted as a youth lightly stepping to the edge of a precipice surrounded by lofty mountains. He looks out into the distance; the abyss at his feet holds no terrors for him. A dog barks at his heels. The wand over his shoulder is a symbol of the will, and the wallet contains the stored-up knowledge of universal memory. The rose he carries is white, to indicate freedom from lower forms of desire.

The Fool is about to enter the supreme adventure —that of passing through the gates of experience to reach Divine Wisdom. He is the cosmic Life-Breath, about to descend into the abyss of manifestation. Every man must journey forward and choose between good and evil. If he has no philosophy, he is The Fool. He must pass through the experiences suggested in the remaining 21 cards, to reach in card 21 the climax of cosmic consciousness or Divine Wisdom.

DIVINATORY MEANING: The subject of the reading faces a choice in life—a choice of vital importance to him. Therefore he must be careful to use all his powers to make the right choice.

REVERSED: The choice made is likely to be faulty.

O

THE FOOL.

KEY I—THE MAGICIAN

DESCRIPTION: The Magician has above his head the cosmic lemniscate shaped like a figure 8 on its side, symbol of eternal life. Above his waist is a serpent devouring its own tail—a well-known symbol of eternity. In his right hand is a wand raised toward heaven, while his left hand points to the earth. He is drawing power from above and directing it into manifestation. On the table are the symbols of the four suits of the Minor Arcana, signifying the natural elements of life: air, fire, water and earth. Roses and lilies in the garden about him show the cultivation of desires. He represents the personal will in its union with the Divine, which then has the knowledge and power to bring things into manifestation through conscious self-awareness.

DIVINATORY MEANING: Will, mastery, skill, occult wisdom, power, diplomacy. The ability to take power from above and direct it through desire into manifestation.

REVERSED: The use of power for destructive ends. Weakness, indecision.

I

THE MAGICIAN.

KEY 2—THE HIGH PRIESTESS

DESCRIPTION: The High Priestess sits with the crescent moon at her feet and on her head a diadem showing the full moon set in two crescent moons. On her breast is a solar cross showing the union of the positive and negative life elements. The scroll in her lap is the Tora (Divine Law); it is only slightly unrolled, for the instruction contained therein is hidden, save for a partial glimpse, from the ordinary human eye. A veil also covers half of the scroll, thus intimating that only one-half of the mystery of being can be comprehended. She sits between the pillars of the positive and negative forces. The black pillar, Boaz, represents the negative life principle; and the white one, Jakin, the positive life principle.

The high priestess is both eternal and the subconscious mind. She is the balancing power between initiative and resistance—thus she sits between the pillars. The veil between the pillars is decorated with pomegranate (female) and palm (male) symbols, indicating that the subconscious is only potentially reproductive. Only when this veil is penetrated by conscious desire can creativity be actualized.

DIVINATORY MEANING: Hidden influences at work, unrevealed future. Creative forces of the subconscious, the female side of the brain at work for the artist, poet, and mystic. A woman of great intuition, inner illumination.

REVERSED: Accepting surface knowledge, sensual enjoyment, conceit.

THE HIGH PRIESTESS

KEY 3—THE EMPRESS

DESCRIPTION: A matronly woman, suggesting one who is about to be a mother, is seated in a fertile garden. Her hair is bound by a wreath of myrtle, symbolizing radiant energy. She wears a crown of 12 stars. The seven pearls around her neck are of Venus; a heart-shaped shield, also symbolic of Venus, rests against her throne.

While the High Priestess symbolizes the virgin state of the cosmic subconsciousness, the Empress typifies the productive, generative activities in the subconscious, after it has been impregnated by seed ideas. She is the symbol of production through the female principle: growth and organization in the natural world; universal fertility; the symbol of the heart (what you believe in your heart).

DIVINATORY MEANING: Marriage, Material wealth, sound understanding; fertility for would-be parents, farmers, or people in the creative arts. In the wrong position with respect to other cards, might indicate dissipation, luxury.

REVERSED: Inaction, frittering away of resources. Poverty may disrupt home; possibility of war and destruction.

THE EMPRESS.

KEY 4—THE EMPEROR

DESCRIPTION: Commanding, stately, he sits on a throne whose arms and back are adorned with rams' heads (emblem of Mars). In his right hand he carries a sceptre in the form of the Egyptian ankh, also called the Crux Ansata—Cross of Life —before which the powers of darkness fall back. The globe in his left hand is the symbol of dominion. On his shoulder is another ram's head. He is seated against a background of stark, bare mountains, representing the sterility of regulation and unyielding power.

This card and that of the Empress do not necessarily denote married life. The Emperor occupies the intellectual throne—the lordship of thought and reason rather than that of the emotions, the subconscious.

DIVINATORY MEANING: Kingship, government, leadership. Control of masses, temporal power. Mental activity; the domination of intelligence over passion.

REVERSED: Emotional immaturity, bondage to parents. Possibility of injury to body or household, of being defrauded out of inheritance.

IV

THE EMPEROR.

KEY 5—THE HIEROPHANT

DESCRIPTION: The master of the sacred mysteries wears the triple crown of a pope, signifying the creative, formative, and material worlds. He holds a sceptre terminating in a triple cross. At his feet are crossed keys, a gold one for solar energy and a silver one for the unseen forces of the moon. The two tonsured priests kneeling before him again indicate duality, for one garment is decorated with the white lilies of spiritual thought and the other with the red roses of desire. He may represent the Pope, but more likely the idea of a pontiff who is master to the masses. He is the ruling power of external religion, whereas the High Priestess teaches only in secret to initiates.

DIVINATORY MEANING: Preference for the outer forms of religion. The need to conform, to be socially approved.

REVERSED: Unconventionality, unorthodoxy, openness to new ideas in any field. Danger of becoming superstitious. Can be the card of the inventor as well as the crackpot.

THE HIEROPHANT

KEY 6—THE LOVERS

DESCRIPTION: The man represents Adam, namer of things; he is also identified with the Magician. The woman is Eve. Above them is the Angel Raphael, who, with arms extended, pours down influence upon them. Behind the man is the Tree of Life, bearing 12 fruits; behind the woman is the Tree of the Knowledge of Good and Evil, with a serpent twining around it.

Eve here is identified with the High Priestess and the Empress. The woman looks at the angel; the man toward the woman. The self-conscious intellect represented by the man does not establish direct contact with superconsciousness (the Angel), except through Eve (the subconscious). This is the card of human love, as part of the way, the truth and the life.

DIVINATORY MEANING: Choice between diverse allurements; the struggle between sacred and profane love. Attraction, beauty, harmony of the inner and outer life. The power of choice means responsibility.

REVERSED: Parental interference, danger of marriage breaking up, quarrels over children. The possibility of wrong choice.

THE LOVERS.

KEY 7—THE CHARIOT

DESCRIPTION: An erect and princely figure rides under a starry canopy in a chariot drawn by two sphinxes. He carries the wand of authority and the will. The shield on the front of the chariot bears a symbol typifying the union of positive and negative forces. The white sphinx is a symbol of mercy; the black one of stern justice.

Both the carnal and spiritual urges are under the strong control of the charioteer. The car symbolizes the combination of heavenly and earthly powers. The human personality is the vehicle through which the self manifests its dominion over all things. He drives the chariot by the strength of his will and the magic wand, but the tension of his will may weaken and the sphinxes may pull in different directions and tear him and his chariot in two.

DIVINATORY MEANING: Conquest, success for those engaged in artistic pursuits, triumph over money difficulties, ill health and foes. Advantage for the seeker will result if he resists his lower promptings and masters his animal passions. It is a card of those who achieve greatness. May also betoken travel in comfort.

REVERSED: Sudden collapse of a project, decadent desires, perhaps an unethical victory, vengeance.

THE CHARIOT.

KEY 8—STRENGTH

DESCRIPITION: A woman over whose head we see the cosmic lemniscate, symbol of eternal life, the same as that shown in the card of the Magician. She is shown confidently closing the lion's mouth. Around her waist is a chain of roses—the union of desires which creates such strength that wild, unconscious force bows before it.

For a consciousness that is aware of the sign of Eternity above it, there are no obstacles, nor can there be any resistance.

DIVINATORY MEANING: Spiritual power overcomes material power. The triumph of love over hate, the higher nature over carnal desires.

REVERSED: The abuse of power, the domination of the material, discord. This card suggests the need for meditation as a help in controlling the animal passions. Key 17 develops this idea further.

VIII

STRENGTH.

KEY 9—THE HERMIT

DESCRIPTION: The Hermit is alone on a snowy mountain peak far above the weary climbers below, for whom he lights the way. His lantern is a six-pointed star, suggesting "Where I am, there you also may be." He is Absolute Wisdom, the goal of existence, while the Fool typifies the same Absolute before manifestation. Consequently Tarot #0 is a youth looking upward in the morning light, while Tarot #9 is a bearded ancient looking down at night. Every practice in occult training aims at the union of personal consciousness with the Cosmic Will which is the cause of all manifestations.

DIVINATORY MEANING: Silent council, wisdom from above, prudence. A meeting with one who will guide the seeker on the path to material or spiritual goals. Attainment. Possible journey.

REVERSED: Immaturity, foolish vices, refusal to grow old, the perpetual Peter Pan.

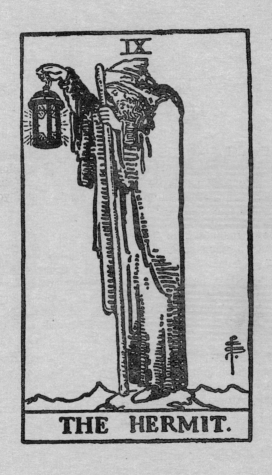

THE HERMIT.

KEY 10—THE WHEEL OF FORTUNE

DESCRIPTION: At the corners of this Tarot are the mystical animals mentioned in the Bible (Ezekiel 1:10, Revelation 4:7). They correspond to the fixed signs of the zodiac: the bull to Taurus; the lion to Leo; the eagle to Scorpio; the man or angel to Aquarius. They typify unchanging reality in relation to the ever-turning wheel. That which was, is, and ever shall be remains the same; rotation of events goes on within it. The laws of cause and effect are always operative.

The evolution of consciousness from lower forms to higher is represented by the jackal-headed Egyptian God, Hermes-Anubis, while on the left side of the wheel the serpent of cosmic energy flows into form. The Sphinx is the equilibrating principle, the eternal self of man behind the veil of personality. The word TARO is interspersed around the wheel with the alchemical signs for mercury (*above*), sulphur (*right*), salt (*left*), and Aquarius, symbol of water (dissolution), below.

DIVINATORY MEANING: Good fortune, success, increase, Unexpected turn of luck.

REVERSED: Fortune will have its ups and downs; there may be a turn for the worse; you will reap as you have sown.

WHEEL of FORTUNE.

KEY 11—JUSTICE

DESCRIPTION: The figure of Justice is seated in front of two pillars, between which is stretched a veil like that in the card of the High Priestess (Key #2). However, while the pillars of the High Priestess open into the realm of the subconscious, the pillars of Justice here open into the superconscious, where all knowledge resides.

The figure is the personification of spiritual justice and therefore wears no blindfold. Her crown carries three turrets and is ornamented with a square jewel. In her left hand, the scales (always related to balanced judgment); in her right, a double-edged sword which cuts two ways, indicating that action is required to penetrate matter and inform it.

DIVINATORY MEANING: A balanced personality. Legal aspects of money matters with good outcome. The elimination of useless, outworn forms of education. A mixture of the right ingredients, as in science, chemistry or cooking. May mean education, with a well-balanced mind as its aim.

REVERSED: Injustice, inequality, legal complications, bias, excessive severity. When this card is near #12, The Hanged Man, it means that the mercy of the Sermon on the Mount should be used rather that the severity of the Ten Commandments.

172

XI

JUSTICE .

KEY 12—THE HANGED MAN

DESCRIPTION: The Hanged Man is suspended from a gallows, a T-cross of living wood, His arms, folded behind his back, together with his head, form a triangle with the point downward; his legs form a cross. Thus the geometrical figure concealed here is that of a cross surmounting a water triangle. There is a nimbus about his head, and his face expresses deep entrancement rather than suffering.

The figure suggests the reversal of the mind rather than of the body. A silent, unostentatious reversal of one's way of life, combined with perfect tolerance of the ways of other people, is the aim of the practical occultist.

DIVINATORY MEANING: Surrender to a higher Being causes a reversal in one's way of life. In spiritual matters, wisdom, prophetic power, self-sacrifice. May also mean suspended decisions, a pause in one's life.

REVERSED: Absorption in physical matters. Preoccupation with the ego. Resistance to spiritual influences, arrogance. False prophecy.

THE HANGED MAN.

KEY 13—DEATH

DESCRIPTION: The mysterious horseman, Death, rides a well-bridled horse, and moves slowly across a field. He bears a black banner emblazoned with the mystic rose, which signifies life. On the edge of the horizon, the sun shines between two towers. All are powerless before the rider—king, child, girl, fall prostrate before him, while a priest awaits his coming with clasped hands.

The card represents the death of the old self—not necessarily physical death. The sloughing off of fleshly desires. He who realizes that death must be conquered by the regeneration of the soul is on the way to attaining eternal life.

DIVINATORY MEANING: Transformation, change. Sometimes destruction followed or preceded by transformation. The change may be in the form of consciousness. Sometimes it may mean birth and renewal.

REVERSED: Temporary stagnation, tendency to inertia.

DEATH.

KEY 14—TEMPERANCE

DESCRIPTION: Michael, angel of the Sun, is seen pouring the essence of life from the silver cup of the subconscious imagination into the golden cup of the conscious. The entry of Spirit into matter. This is what the Fool must learn on his path to mastery. The symbol on his breast, a square with a triangle within, is the sign of the sacred book of the Tarot. This refers to the seven aspects of divine life and also the seven chakras. One of the angel's feet rests on the earth and the other in the water, to show that he is equally at home in both the conscious and subconscious aspects of life. The irises blooming on the bank are symbols of the Greek goddess of the rainbow.

DIVINATORY MEANING: Good management. What we have imagined can be brought forth. Working in harmony with others, coordination.

REVERSED: Competing interests in business or personal affairs. Inability to coordinate the imagination with the material manifestation. Quarreling, separation.

TEMPERANCE.

KEY 15—THE DEVIL

DESCRIPTION: A horned devil with wings like those of a bat sits on a half-cube which signifies the half-knowledge of only the visible, sensory side of existence. His right hand is upraised; an inverted flaming torch, symbolic of black magic and destruction, is in his left. On his forehead, the inverted pentagram between his horns shows that man's place in the universe is here reversed. From a ring in the half-cube, chains are carried to the necks of a man and a woman. The chains are loose enough to be slipped off, suggesting that much of bondage is imaginary.

The Devil is the opposite of the Angel (Key #6). The man and woman are bestialized reproductions of those shown in the same card.

DIVINATORY MEANING: Domination of matter over spirit. Sensation divorced from understanding. Illness, bondage to the material, violence, revolution, extraordinary effort, force. Black magic.

REVERSED: The beginning of spiritual understanding. A physical healing has started. Tendency to ineffectuality, indecision.

THE DEVIL.

181

KEY 16—THE TOWER

DESCRIPTION: Struck by lightning issuing from the sun, the crown of materialistic thought falls from the tower. The falling drops of light seen here, as well as in Key #18 and in the Aces of three suits of the Minor Arcana (Wands, Cups and Swords), are Hebrew "Yods." They signify the descent of the life force from above into the conditions of material existence. The lightning flash represents the same power as that which is drawn from above by the Magician and which lights the Hermit's lantern. It is Spiritual Truth, which breaks down ignorance and false reasoning.

The Tower is only one of several titles that have been given to this card. Among them are "The Lightning-Struck Tower" and "The House of God." The card suggests the breaking down of existing forms in order to make room for new ones. In terms of consciousness, the lightning flash also symbolizes the brilliant, momentary glimpse of truth. The crown on the top of the tower symbolizes the materialistic concept of life—shown as it is thrust from power.

DIVINATORY MEANING: Overthrow of existing modes of life. Conflict, unforeseen catastrophe. Old notions upset; disruption that may bring enlightenment in its wake. Selfish ambition about to fall, bankruptcy.

REVERSED: Oppression, imprisonment. The same as above in lesser degree.

THE TOWER.

KEY 17—THE STAR

DESCRIPTION: An eight-pointed star signifying radiant cosmic energy and surrounded by seven smaller stars, radiates solar energy on the young girl kneeling on the land, her right foot upon the water. She pours the Waters of Life impartially from two ewers into the pool of universal consciousness and onto the earth—which represents matter. The bird is the soul resting in the tree of life.

The Maiden is eternal youth and beauty. She is Mother Nature and is identified with the Empress and the High Priestess, as well as with the woman in Key #8 who tames the lion. The card represents the Waters of Life flowing freely and perpetually renewing creation.

DIVINATORY MEANING: Hope, courage, inspiration. No destruction is final. Unselfish aid will be given. Good health. Spiritual love.

REVERSED: Stubbornness, pessimism, doubt.

THE STAR.

KEY 18—THE MOON

DESCRIPTION: A dog and a wolf are seen baying at the moon. The pool in the foreground is the same as that shown in Keys #14 and #17. It is the great deep of mind stuff out of which emerges physical manifestation. The shellfish symbolizes the early stages of conscious unfoldment. The wolf is nature's untamed creation, while the dog is a product of adaptation to life with man. The path ascends ever upward between the towers.

The upward progress of man is here symbolized; the moon signifies the reflected light of subconsciousness; the falling drops of dew (Yods) represent the descent of the life-force from above into material existence.

DIVINATORY MEANING: Imagination, intuition, dreams. May mean bad luck to one you love. Unforeseen perils, deception, secret foes.

REVERSED: Storms will be weathered, peace gained at a cost. Imagination will be harnessed by practical considerations.

THE MOON.

KEY 19—THE SUN

DESCRIPTION: A naked child mounted on a white horse holds a banner aloft. The child rides without saddle or bridle because he represents perfect balance and control between the self-conscious and the unconscious. He seems to have emerged from the walled garden behind him into the glorious sunlight. Four sunflowers, corresponding to the four kingdoms of nature—mineral, vegetable, animal and human—are turned toward the child, signifying that all creation turns to man for its final development.

Creativeness, life forever renewed. Nature, the mother of all growth and life.

DIVINATORY MEANING: Attainment and material happiness. Good marriage and happy reunions. Achievements in art, science and agriculture. Studies completed, liberation; pleasure in the simple life.

REVERSED: Future plans clouded; possible broken engagement; loss of a valued object unless vigilance is exerted; voided contract.

THE SUN .

KEY 20—JUDGMENT

DESCRIPTION: The angel Gabriel emerges from the heavens, blowing on his bannered trumpet. This imperious blast is the creative Word which liberates man from his terrestial limitations. The dead are rising from their coffins which are floating on the sea. A man, a woman and between them a child. They raise their arms in adoration and ecstasy. Snowy mountains in the background represent the heights of abstract thought.

This is the reawakening of nature under the influence of the spirit, the mystery of birth in death.

DIVINATORY MEANING: Awakening, change of position, renewal. A change in personal consciousness which is now on the verge of blending with the universal.

REVERSED: Failure to find happiness in old age. Fear of death. Separation and disillusionment. Weakness. Physical health must be watched. Possible loss of worldly goods.

JUDGEMENT.

KEY 21—THE WORLD

DESCRIPTION: A wreath of leaves surrounds the dancer, who holds in each hand a magic wand. The four corners of the card show the four animals of Ezekiel and the Apocalypse. This is a slightly different version from that in Key #10.

The wreath symbolizes Nature on her regular course, and also the crown of the initiate, which is given to those who master the four guardians and thus enter into the presence of unveiled Truth. The dancer represents the final attainment of man, the merging of the self-conscious with the subconscious and blending these two with superconsciousness. This card implies the state of cosmic consciousness, the final goal to which all the other cards have led.

DIVINATORY MEANING: Completion, reward, assured success. Triumph in all undertakings. Arrival at the state of cosmic consciousness. Can mean also movement in one's affairs, travel.

REVERSED: Fear of change. Earthbound spirit attached to one place or profession. Sloth and stubbornness. Refusal to learn the lessons of life as shown in the other cards.

THE WORLD.

4.

DIVINATION BY TAROT CARDS

Before attempting to make divinations, it is wise to learn the meanings of all 78 cards. These should be memorized, since the subconscious mind seems to direct the shuffling of the cards and their subsequent laying out, and if you have not mastered their meanings, your results will be less satisfactory.

There are many different packs of Tarot cards on the market at the present time. Most of the new packs have been done according to the artist's personal imagination and seem to range far from the original meanings. An example is the pack found in the book, *Salvador Dali's Tarot*. Michael Pollack, the author, tries to interpret the fanciful, offbeat drawings, but the results are not for a serious interpretation. There are also reprints of older decks but they too, while interesting and quaint, do not come up to the easy-to-understand Rider pack. These are the cards I have used in this book. They were drawn buy the well-known English artist Pamela Coleman Smith under the direction of Arthur Edward Waite and used in his book, *The Pictorial Key to the Tarot*. This was first printed in 1910 in England and it has been popular ever since. The book's subtitle tells it all: "Being Fragments of a Secret Tradition under the Veil of Divination."

Keep your cards wrapped in a piece of silk, or in a small box of their own to protect their vibrations. Do not let others use your cards or handle them—except the seeker when you are giving a reading. Even then, if you prefer, it is sufficient for the seeker to place his hands on the deck while thinking of his question, leaving the entire process of shuffling to you.

Make your mind as passive as possible when shuffling and laying out the cards. Do not try to guess their meanings; go by what has been worked out for you in this book. There are special circumstances of divination, however, when the meanings given may be modified or expanded.

While the subject is shuffling the cards, with his mind concentrated on the question he wants answered, the reader must quietly ask that only the highest spiritual forces surround the procedure, and that the answers given by the cards will be of a constructive and helpful nature. The readers asks that he will be guided to interpret them correctly and be so illuminated as to give positive help to the seeker.

In a reading, glance quickly at all the cards after you have laid them out, and try to get a general impression as to whether they are, on the whole, encouraging or not; whether the question has to do with money and business affairs, love and family relations, states of mind and spirit, etc. Then go back and read each card carefully, checking with the meanings given in this book. Try to make a running story out of what you read in the cards, letting your intuition play its part.

If after laying out the cards by either of the suggested methods and reading them, the seeker says they do not answer his specific question, ask him if the cards have answered other, perhaps deeper, questions the seeker has not actually formulated but which had been in his mind. It often happens that the cards seem to ignore the superficial question asked and go beneath it to deeper problems that have recently been a constant source of anxiety to the subject.

If the cards do not seem to fall right, ask the subject to shuffle again, concentrating on his question more carefully. If they still do not make sense, it would be well to put the reading off for another day.

A professional Tarot card reader never finishes a reading on a discouraging note, so please do the same. If the overall reading seems negative, then indicate to the seeker how he or she can overcome his or her problems by work, study, application to tasks, taking better care of health, and by expending more love and compassion on relationships. Never predict a serious illness or a death, no matter what the cards seem to say.

Your reading could tip the scales towards a positive or negative frame of mind in the seeker. Therefore, when you do a reading you take on the responsibility of guiding the person's life by your suggestions. Make them always helpful and positive.

Reading the Tarot is a responsibility that should not be taken lightly. It gives you the opportunity to help others gain an insight into what may be holding them back from their fullest self-expression. Other people are as sensitive as you are, and giving a discouraging reading with no hope held out for the future is a cruel and pointless thing to do. What you say can color the seeker's future life; indeed, I have known several cases where it did just that, with diastrous results. We have all seen seemingly hopeless lives suddenly take remarkable turns for the better with just a small amount of encouragement.

Memorize the meanings of the cards and make them into a running story. If you cannot fit a card into the story, just say so, and maybe the seeker himself can do so. Use a combination of good sense and intuition, and you will be delighted to see how helpful you can be to others with a pack of cards!

I. The Ancient Celtic Method *

The very first step is for you, the reader, to select from the deck the COURT CARD to represent the subject of the reading, as follows:

If the subject has:

    Blonde hair and blue eyes, select a WAND
    Light brown hair and hazel eyes, a CUP
    Dark brown hair and brown eyes, a SWORD
    Black hair and very dark eyes, a PENTACLE

For a man, select a KING in the proper suit; for a woman, a QUEEN; for a young man, a KNIGHT; for a youth or child (male or female), a PAGE.

Second step:

Now place this card in front of you, face upward. It is called the SIGNIFICATOR.

---

* I have chosen, among many methods of divination, the two described here, because I have found them the most easily mastered and the most rewarding.

Third step:

Ask the subject to shuffle the rest of the deck, suggesting that it be very thoroughly done so that some of the pictures will be reversed.

As the subject shuffles, tell him that it is important for him to concentrate on the question he wants answered. This question can be spoken aloud to the reader or left unspoken.

Fourth step:

After shuffling, ask the subject to cut the pack into three piles toward the left, with the left hand.

Fifth step:

Now you, the reader pick up the deck with your left hand, toward the left, always keeping the cards face downward.

Sixth step:

Turn up the top or FIRST CARD. Cover the SIGNIFICATOR with it and say, "THIS COVERS HIM."

The FIRST CARD represents the general atmosphere that surrounds the question asked; the influences at work around it.

Seventh step:

Turn up the SECOND CARD and lay it across the FIRST, saying, "THIS CROSSES HIM." This card, lying on its side, is always read as right side up, not reversed.

The SECOND CARD shows what the opposing forces may be, for good or evil.

Eighth step:

Turn up the THIRD CARD and place it below the SIGNIFICATOR, saying, "THIS IS BENEATH HIM."

The THIRD CARD shows the foundation or basis of the matter; something that has already become part of the subject's experience.

Ninth step:

Turn up the FOURTH CARD; place it on the left side of the SIGNIFICATOR, saying, "THIS IS BEHIND HIM."

The FOURTH CARD shows the influence that has just passed or is now passing away.

Tenth step:

Turn up the FIFTH CARD; place it directly above the SIGNIFICATOR, saying, "THIS CROWNS HIM."

The FIFTH CARD represents an influence that *may* come into being.

Eleventh step:

Turn up the SIXTH CARD; place it on the right side of the SIGNIFICATOR, saying, "THIS IS BEFORE HIM."

The SIXTH CARD shows the influence that will operate in the near future.

Twelfth step:

(The cards are now disposed in the form of a cross, with the SIGNIFICATOR, covered by the FIRST CARD and crossed by the SECOND CARD, in the center.)

Now turn up the next four cards in succession and place them in a straight line, one above the other, on the right-hand side of the cross.

The first of these four cards, that is to say, the SEVENTH CARD, represents the negative feelings, the fears, the subject has on the matter.

The second of the four cards, the EIGHTH CARD,

represents the subject's environment, the
and influence of family and friends.

The third of these cards, the NINTH CAR
resents the subject's own hopes and ideals
matter.

The last of the cards, the TENTH CARD, tells the
outcome of the matter—the cumulative result of the
influences exerted by the other cards. It should in-
clude all that has been divined from the other cards
on the table.

The process is now completed, but should it
happen that the last card is of a doubtful nature,
from which no final conclusion can be drawn, it
may be well to repeat the entire operation, taking
the TENTH CARD as the SIGNIFICATOR, instead of the one previously used. The pack should
again be thoroughly shuffled by the subject, cut
three times, and the ten cards laid out by the reader
as before. By this means, a more detailed account
of the outcome may be obtained.

Here are a few additional suggestions for the
student's guidance. If the majority of the cards in
the layout come from the Major Arcana, there is
a strong indication that there are powerful outside
forces at work on the subject's affairs. If there are
several Court cards in a layout, it may indicate: if
Wands, a business conference; if Cups, gay com-
pany; if Swords, conflict; if Pentacles, politics. Two
Kings may also indicate a conference; two Queens
facing each other, gossip; two Knights, a fight; two
Pages, playful pastimes. If, in any reading, the
TENTH CARD should be a Court card, this shows
that the outcome of the matter may be subject to
another's will or authority and that what happens to
the questioner depends to a great extent upon this
other person.

DIAGRAM I

THE ANCIENT CELTIC METHOD

Significator is
placed in center.

No. 1   This covers him.

No. 2   This crosses him.

No. 3   This is beneath him.

No. 4   This is behind him.

Significator
plus card No. 1

No. 5   This crowns him.

No. 6   This is before him.

No. 7   What he fears.

No. 8   Family opinion.

No. 9   His hopes.

No. 10   Final outcome.

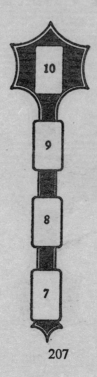

A Specimen Reading by the Celtic Method

Note: The student should go through his own deck and pick out the cards corresponding to those listed below and place them in the proper position before he attempts to follow the history of the reading given below. Then he should compare what has been indicated here with what he would have said if these cards came up in a reading he was giving.

FIRST, the QUEEN OF SWORDS was chosen as the SIGNIFICATOR. (The subject was a brown-haired, brown-eyed woman).
THE QUESTION ASKED BY THE SUBJECT: "Will I have material security in my later years?" (The subject has not told the reader what she is asking).

FIRST CARD—The aura surrounding the question. NINE OF CUPS (Divinatory meaning: material success, assured future).
Reader's comment: "It would seem from this card

that your question is about material success or well-being."

SECOND CARD—The opposing forces.
FIVE OF PENTACLES (Material trouble, loneliness, destitution).
Reader's comment: "The opposing force to your well-being seems to be a fear of destitution and loneliness."

THIRD CARD—The basis of the matter; what has already been experienced.
SEVEN OF SWORDS (Partial success, unstable efforts).
Reader's comment: "In your past there seems to have been some loss of property or status, but something was saved from the situation.

FOURTH CARD—Influence that has just passed.
SEVEN OF CUPS (Castles in the air; insubstantial dreams).
Reader's comment: "It looks as if you had been scattering your forces; as if you had difficulty concentrating on any one project."

FIFTH CARD—The influence that *may* come into being.
FOUR OF PENTACLES (Loss of possessions, if one is not vigilant).
Reader's comment: "There is a possibility of further reverses."

SIXTH CARD—The influence that will operate in the near future.
   WHEEL OF FORTUNE (Unexpected luck, increase, success).
Reader's comment: This card seems to counteract the influence of some of the preceding ones and directs you toward the path of success.

SEVENTH CARD—The subject's fears on the matter.
   THE MOON, Reversed (Imagination harnessed by practical considerations).
Reader's comment: Most likely you have been worried about your impracticality. This card indicates that a previous flightiness is now under better control.

EIGHTH CARD—Opinions of friends and relatives.
   JUDGMENT, Reversed. (Possible loss of worldly goods.)
Reader's comment: Your friends think you may sustain losses and that you should exercise more care. They are afraid you will make the same mistakes you once made.

NINTH CARD—Your own hopes.
   KING OF CUPS (Bachelor, friendly, creative man disposed in favor of the subject.)
Reader's comment: "Looks as if a man is going to be helpful to you in the fulfillment of your hopes."

TENTH CARD—Total influence of all cards.
THREE OF CUPS (The conclusion of the matter in plenty).

Reader's comment: "You have had serious doubts of your future happiness, based on what you and your friends have thought of as your flightiness, impracticality. But due to a certain amount of effort on your part to overcome this, as well as certain chance factors in your favor, including the help of a man who may be counselor, adviser, friend—there should be a happy answer to your question."

II. The Tree of Life Method*

1) Choose the appropriate card to represent the subject, as in the CELTIC METHOD. This card is placed high in the center of the table. It is the SIGNIFICATOR.

2) Ask the subject to shuffle the deck for himself and to put into the process all his hopes and fears, questions and desires.

3) Have the subject cut the pack into three parts toward the left with his left hand.

4) Now lay out the first nine cards in three triangles below the SIGNIFICATOR, as shown in *Diagram II.*

* The above is my own simplified verson, for the beginner, of a method of reading a full life history.

213

TRIANGLE 1 (pointing upward) represents spirituality, the highest ideal of the subject.

TRIANGLE 2 (pointing downward) represents the intellectual and moral nature of the subject.

TRIANGLE 3 (pointing downward) represents the subject's subconsciousness—his intuition, desires and impulses.

FIRST CARD (top, center)—the subject's highest intelligence

SECOND CARD (right base of Triangle 1)—creative force, the "father" card.

THIRD CARD (left base of Triangle 1)—life, wisdom, the "mother" card.

FOURTH CARD (right base of Triangle 2)—virtues, good qualities.

FIFTH CARD (left base of Triangle 2)—conquest, intellectual or physical force.

SIXTH CARD (apex of inverted Triangle 2)—spirit of sacrifice, health.

SEVENTH CARD (right base of Triangle 3)—Venus, love, lust.

EIGHTH CARD (left base of Triangle 3)—procreation, arts, crafts.

NINTH CARD (at the apex of Triangle 3)—imagination, creative mental and physical forces.

TENTH CARD is placed directly below the apex of Triangle 3. It represents the physical body or the earthly home.

5) Place a reserve deck of the next 7 cards from the pack face down at the extreme left. (All other cards have been placed face up.)

This is called the Daath, or qualifying, pack, and it is to be read only after all the other cards have been interpreted. It stands for all that is still in a state of unfolding, the immediate future of the subject.

It will be noted that the cards in the diagram form three branches of the Tree of Life. The cards that fall in the left branch should be interpreted uncompromisingly, strictly. Those in the center are interpreted in a spirit of moderation and compromise; those in the right-hand branch, in a spirit of love and compassion.

One experienced in the art of divination may attempt a complete LIFE reading by using the entire pack and leaving the significator in the pack. Then 7 cards are laid out in the 10 places, instead of one card in each, and the Daath pack contains 8 cards. The complete layout is done three times—once for the past, once for the present and once again for the future. This complete Tree of Life should not be done oftener than once a year for the subject.

Example of a Reading by the Tree of Life Method

The reading I have chosen for an illustration of the Tree of Life method is that of a young man of my acquaintance. He was not able to be present, and I myself shuffled the cards, asking for indications as to what was going on in his present life and what might come about for him in the near future.

In order that you may follow the reading more readily, I suggest that you take your own deck of cards and select and arrange the cards exactly according to my layout. It may be helpful for you to consult the Tree of Life diagram.

The first ten cards in my reading were as follows:

No. 1 Page of
Wands
(Reversed)

No. 2 Three of
Swords
(Reversed)

No. 3 Eight of
Swords

No. 4 The Empress

No. 5 Ten of Cups
(Reversed)

No. 6 Ace of
Pentacles

No. 7 Five of
Swords

No. 8 Two of Cups

No. 9 Nine of
Swords
(Reversed)

No. 10 Ten of
Wands

In the qualifying or Daath pack of seven cards, I found the following:

JUDGMENT, THREE OF PENTACLES, FOUR OF CUPS, THE CHARIOT, THE HANGED MAN, THE KING OF WANDS AND THE TEN OF SWORDS (REV.)

(Note how many Swords occur in this layout. Before we go any further, we note that this indicates trouble and a great deal of activity.)

Now we arrange the cards as in the chart.

TRIANGLE #1 THE SOUL Cards #1, 2 and 3 (in the Triangle of Spirituality) all betoken loss, disorder, indecision, instability and perhaps censure of self. The young man is definitely unhappy and confused.

TRIANGLE #2 THE REASON The next 3 cards are arranged in the Triangle of Reason. At the right-hand apex of the triangle (where qualities and virtues are shown) is Card #4, the Empress, expressing material wealth and sound understanding. This card indicates that in spite of confusion, the subject has sound understanding, is reasonable and full of mercy. Card #5 (the Ten of Cups, reversed) shows loss of friendship and love. Card #6 (the Ace of Pentacles) is a card of material gain and, since it is an Ace, it shows the young man is at the beginning of prosperity. In this triangle, we have two cards of material gain and one of spiritual loss, perhaps occasioned by the loss of a loved one.

TRIANGLE #3 THE EMOTIONS .The next three cards (in the Triangle of intuition, feelings, desires, impulses) show card #7 on the right apex of the triangle. It is the Five of Swords (Rev.) which can be read as loss or defeat. Since it lies in the location of Venus and Love, we read it as loss of love. Card #8, on the left side of the triangle, is the Two of Cups, denoting love, passion and friendship. The position of the card in the triangle, however, indicates arts or crafts, and we read it, therefore as love of creative work. Card #9, the Nine of Swords (Rev.), is the card of the imagination. It reveals that the young man is filled with doubt and shame, and again it is in the realm of love.

The *10th card* in the layout—by itself at the bottom of the center pillar is the Ten of Wands. This place in the layout represents either home or the body, and, since there has been no indication of physical illness in the other cards, we must assume that his burden is connected with home or an impending breakdown in marriage.

THE QUALIFYING PACK Now we come to the qualifying or Daath pack of seven cards, and the interpretation thereof.

JUDGMENT: The spirit of the young man regains possession of itself; there will be a renewal and as this card is next to

THE THREE OF PENTACLES: The renewal will come about through his skill and mastery in his art or craft.

THE FOUR OF CUPS: This betokens a slight weariness and dissatisfaction with the subject's new material success. He may be longing for a love relationship that will be as successful as his career promises to be.

THE CHARIOT: This suggests that he is keeping himself under control mentally, physically and emotionally.

THE HANGED MAN: This card indicates that he is learning wisdom in spiritual matters.

THE KING OF WANDS (Reversed): This usually represents an enterprising man, honest and conscientious, and suggests that the subject is being rather severe with himself, as he learns the difficult lesson of self-discipline.

THE TEN OF SWORDS (Reversed): This card points to advantage, success and favor, but these may not be permanent and special vigilance must be exercised to preserve them.

Dear J......L......:

I'm sorry you could not have been with me when I read the Tarot cards, after you had asked on the telephone for some illumination as to your present state of mind. But as I promised, I will give you a brief summary of what the cards conveyed—after I had laid them out in the Tree of Life method. I must say that there are conflicting indications in the way the cards fell. It seems clear that you are going

220

through a somewhat undecided and troubled time. Although you are on the threshold of possible success and material gain, you are held back by some spiritual loss—perhaps the loss of a loved one. Everything indicates that you are intensely creative, imaginative—but that now you are going through a period of self-doubt—possibly because of the breakdown of a marriage? Your present promise of material success does not satisfy you, because you are longing for a love relationship that will be equally successful. But it seems that you are keeping your distress under splendid control and learning wisdom in spiritual matters.

Would you mind a small word of advice from a friend? Since the reading points to advantage, success and favor for you, it seems to me that you will have to have more than the usual self-discipline and special vigilance to hold on to what is promised and to emerge from the negative recent experience. I have confidence that you will do this.

DIAGRAM II
THE TREE OF LIFE METHOD

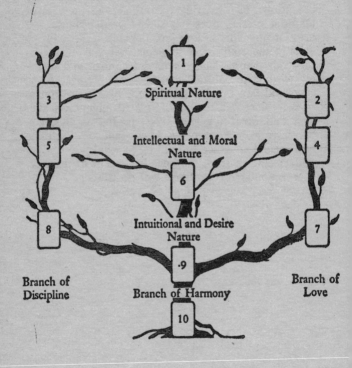

Spiritual Nature

Intellectual and Moral
Nature

Intuitional and Desire
Nature

Branch of
Discipline

Branch of Harmony

Branch of
Love

Daath
Pack

5.

MEDITATION

One of the most important aspects of the Tarot is its power to evoke thought. Eliphas Levi in his book, "Transcendental Magic," has this to say: "The practical value of the Tarot is truly marvelous. A person devoid of books, had he only a Tarot of which he knew how to make use, could in a few years acquire a universal science, and converse with an unequalled doctrine and inexhaustible eloquence."

The purposes of studying the Tarot are many and varied. It can be used for exercising the mind, accustoming it to new and wider concepts, to meditation in a world of higher dimensions. The understanding of the symbols reveals that they are universal in meaning and found everywhere.

Man, as he really is, and as he eternally has been, is a spiritual being. The existence of the physical body does not change the truth of that statement—even though the senses hold man under a hypnotic spell, and he confounds his true self with the life of his physical body. Indeed, man's Self—his true nature, has been buried under so many material wrappings, that it has become a deep, hidden secret.

Those who look for facts in this book will find

them, and if they look hard, they will also find the soul of these facts. Here you will find a great challenge to think for yourself—for the Tarot is both a scientific and reverent subject, and the correct approach to it is with an impartial love of Truth for its own sake and not for the purpose of confirming or refuting any particular theory. The hidden messages that lie here are, to me, in line with the philosophic Truths of all time.

Go deep within in meditation; find your own divine center, and you will understand by direct intuition that which the Tarot only hints at—that which the mystics and philosophers who first designed the cards have been trying to convey to you in these picture-symbols. Prepare to pass through the beautiful gate of symbolism into the starry world beyond.

I suggest that you devote some time to concentrating on each of the twenty-two cards of the Major Arcana, pondering their meaning in relation to yourself and your world.

Physical stillness is the gateway to spiritual illumination. Find a quiet spot, a comfortable chair; do not lie down, or you may doze instead of reaching that state of alertness that you are after. Take this book with you, and choose a picture from the Major Arcana to meditate upon.

Let us take, for example, #8, STRENGTH. Here we have the figure of a woman closing a lion's mouth. Note the high mountains in the background. If you don't know what mountains signify, look it up in the glossary at the end of the book. Look up the meaning of "lion," too; the meaning of the "cosmic lemniscate" over the woman's head; "roses" —decide if they are red or white.

Now that you have delved into the symbolism in the picture and understand that the woman depicts spiritual strength overcoming brute force, think back into your life and remember occasions when brute force was pitted against brute force, and other occasions when love and understanding were used instead. Think back into history to the lives of great men and women, and decide if they used spiritual power to overcome the difficult situations in which they found themselves. Hold your attention to this mode of thinking, and savor each impression before you go on to the next.

The next step is to say to yourself, "I've thought about this with my mind, my intellect; now I am going to let the Divine Self within me, at the very center of my being, reveal its meaning still further." Wait quietly for the "still, small voice" to make itself manifest, to give you further revelation. If your mind wanders, bring it gently back to the listening attitude. It is as if you rang a doorbell and were now waiting patiently for the Divine Self to appear. You may not receive any definite answer or clarification the first time you do this, but if you persist, are not in a hurry, you will be rewarded with whole new vistas of spiritual understanding. A calmness and a peace will steal over you that you can carry out into the turmoil of life—a secret, sacred something that will help you live in the midst of the world, yet not of it, calm and poised from your Divine Center.

A further example of a Tarot to take into meditation is #6, THE LOVERS. Look up the symbolism. Get the understanding that the three figures are the three selves of you—the man representing your conscious everyday mind, the woman your subconscious and the angel your Oversoul or Divine Mind. Note how the man looks to the woman and the woman to the angel. This is to show that your outer mind cannot make contact directly with your Divine Self, but must do so through the subconscious. Do you begin to see why meditation is so important? Why the outer mind must be stilled? The angel is there all the time hovering over the man, but this does him no good unless he is willing to turn within and deliberately search out the contact. When you have done this, ask your angel-self for more wisdom. You first must make the conscious effort for the contact, then comes the subconscious reaction to your conscious effort.

Each one of the twenty-one cards of the Major Arcana, plus Tarot #0, THE FOOL, can be meditated upon many times in this manner, and from this meditation you will gradually find your knowledge of yourself and the world around you greatly enlarging with each period you have devoted to this purpose.

Lay out the cards in pairs: #1 with #0, 2 with 21, 3 with 20, and so on, down to 11 with 12. You will see that THE FOOL (#0) is unconditioned mind stuff, while THE MAGICIAN (#1) is the superman using the mind to create. THE HIGH PRIESTESS (#2) is hidden knowledge, and THE WORLD (#21) is the object of knowledge. THE EMPRESS (#3) is Nature, and JUDGMENT (#20) is Nature eternally reawakening. THE EMPEROR (#4) is the life-bearing principle, and THE SUN (#19) is the eternal life-giver. THE HIEROPHANT (#5) is religion in the outward sense of ritual, while THE MOON (#18) is the realm of the intuition and the inner mysteries.

THE LOVERS (#6) is the spiritual side of love, and THE STAR (#17), the spiritual side of Nature. THE CHARIOT (#7) is man in complete control of his environment, while THE TOWER (#16) shows the overthrow of the materialist. STRENGTH (#8) is the card of spiritual strength over the material, and its complete opposite is shown in THE DEVIL (#15), where black magic has its temporary sway. THE HERMIT (#9) depicts the search for the highest wisdom, which cannot be learned except through tempering and modifying the emotions, as in TEMPERANCE (#14).

THE WHEEL OF FORTUNE (#10) and its opposite card, DEATH (#13), are one—for death only indicates the turning of the wheel. JUSTICE (#11) is truth and wisdom, and THE HANGED MAN (#12) is he who has submitted to ultimate wisdom.

Do you begin to see the many ways in which the Tarot can be meditated upon, and how it blends with all philosophies of all time? It is a most rewarding study, for it pictures the eternal Truths of God, and the Universe in endless variety.

You will begin to have a firm philosophy of your own, based on the eternal Truths so beautifully revealed in the Tarot for those who will take the time to search. Your new philosophy will help you deal with people and life situations that you would have previously found difficult to handle. You will take courage from the fact that you are following in the footsteps of the wise men of all ages, and this will give you a firm foundation for judgment tempered always with the mercy of the Sermon on the Mount.

The stake, the gallows and the rack once waited for the spiritual advanced thinkers who dared to utter thoughts such as those hidden in the Tarot. Hence the pictures and their guarded symbology that even allowed them for centuries to be the gambling cards of Mediterranean peoples and at the same time the book of all knowledge for those who had the secret key.

Now in our more enlightened days these highest truths can be revealed without fear of the hanging rope or the torture rack. So the once complicated mysteries are now being set before those truth-seekers who are willing to seek and delve and meditate to find the inner meanings once again.

We who have had first-hand experience of the amazing potentialities of meditation are ready to meet the doubter and free him from his conception that man is nothing more than his material body.

If he still insists on keeping his eyes shut to the possibilities of man's life here and now, he will have no excuse for the spiritual darkness in which he finds himself.

"O I could sing such grandeurs and glories
        about you!
You have not known what you are, you have
        slumbered upon yourself all your life.
The mockeries are not you;
Underneath them and within them I see you
        lurk,
Whoever you are, claim your own."

—From Walt Whitman's poem, TO YOU.

6.

TAROT FOR THE NEW AGE

A number of years ago I lived in New York City and had a metaphysical bookstore called Inspiration House. I carried a variety of inspirational books, including those on astrology and the I Ching, but I did not know about the Tarot at that time. Then I began to notice that almost every day a customer would ask about this subject. Finally someone filled me in on this fascinating method of divination, which is at the same time a penetrating philosophy.

I ordered the few books available in English and learned where I could obtain some decks of corresponding cards. Many who bought the books came back a few weeks later and said they could not make head or tail of the Tarot, and, truthfully, neither could I!

Up near Mt. Kisco, in Westchester County, New York, I had a small cottage by a lake where I went for weekends. A friend, Jean, often went up there with me, and we spent long winter weekends studying the Tarot books and laying out the cards over and over again until we began to make some sense of them. We were delighted at the subtle symbolism in the drawings and also the deep spiritual inspiration to be found in them.

Soon, when customers complained about the difficulty of understanding the Tarot, I was able to clarify the meanings for them. This led to classes, which I gave first in New York City and later in Florida. It became obvious that I should put what I had learned into a book, for the only ones available at the time were obscure translations from the French or written in very stilted, outdated English.

These contained a number of errors put there on purpose to confuse the uninitiated, erroneous clues so that they could not find the inner Truth.

But we are living in the New Age now, and all Truth is open to those who come with a humble wish to learn and who will not abuse the cosmic laws.

So this book, *The Tarot Revealed*, was written in the simplest form in order that those fresh to the subject could grasp its meaning easily and lay out the cards to get a reasonably accurate reading.

I am particularly fascinated by the Major Arcana, for it seems to give both practical and spiritual instruction for living and the good life. It starts with the Fool, who represents our unconditioned Self, the soul about to step down into manifestation on the earth plane.

Key 1, the Magician, shows how we, magicians all, can reach up into the realms of the unseen and bring down into manifestation our creative ideas. The way the Magician is drawn seems to me incorrect. His left, the receiving hand, should be raised; with the right hand he creates in the material realm.

Key 2, the High Priestess, indicates the subtle influences of our subconscious mind and its great power over our thoughts and, if we permit, our lives. Key 4, the Emperor, shows us the latent power of the conscious mind to direct and create the kind of outer life we desire. Key 3, the Empress, is Nature in her abundance when we are willing to work with her laws and not abuse them. I like the fact that Key 11, Justice, has her eyes open and her justice is therefore not blind. She gives balanced judgment. In fact, all the cards indicate a need for balance in our lives. They urge us, as we travel through life, to choose a middle path with the accent on the spiritual, rather than the material, side.

The Hanged Man, Key 12, is one of my favorite cards, for his symbolism is particularly inspiring. He has reversed his way of life. No longer does he pit his will against the odds; instead he has turned to Spirit and says: "Not my will but Thine be done." Symbols are a universal language because they make cosmic ideas visible to the individual without the need for words. The mystic seeks a silent truth more deeply understood than the words of any language.

Key 5, the Hierophant, is a symbol of organized religion, which we can choose to work with or ignore. The next few keys are like schoolteachers, guiding us so we can avoid the many pitfalls of life. In Key 6, the Lovers, we are warned of the struggle between love and sex. In Key 7, the Chariot, the rider could as well be in a racing car or on a motorcycle. In all cases he must learn to balance his energies, and not let his passions run away with him. The driver here has balanced both the light and dark forces of his nature, symbolized by the two sphinxes. Key 8, Strength, is again an admonition to learn to close the lion's jaws of raw emotion with love instead of force.

By Key 9, the Hermit, we are gaining wisdom, perhaps from a holy man or guru, or through books or meditation. And yet we have not learned all our lessons, for in Key 10, the Wheel of Fortune, we are again shown the possibility of life's ups and downs and warned not to get caught up in them. If we are on the spiritual path, the idea will occur to us to reverse our material way of life and spend more time in meditation and study, to listen to the "still, small voice" and to follow Jesus' commandment to love our neighbor as ourselves.

In Key 13, Death, there is the destruction of the old and the rebirth of the new on a more ideal level. Only the amateur reads this as a card of death. As I have said before, the reader never gives the seeker any outright bad news! He may throw out hints, such as "common sense, moderation, and good judgment can and do overcome negative situations." The soul on its journey through life is learning the lessons of tempering and balancing. This same theme is seen again in Key 14, Temperance, as Michael, one of the archangels, pours the essence of life from the silver cup of the subconscious into the golden cup of the material and conscious. The irises at the water's edge are symbols of the Greek goddess of the rainbow.

The geniuses who first composed the Tarot were certainly conversant with the many forms of religion as well as mythology and used them all to form a composite picture book of the ancient beliefs of mankind. Some may have been lost along the way, but many are alive in our everyday life, as well as those hidden deep in the subconscious of the human race.

What is most interesting about Key 15, the Devil, is that the chains binding the man and woman to the half-cube of half-knowledge are loose, and they can be slipped off whenever they wish. This is true of all of us. Never believe that we are eternally in bondage to anything or anyone of evil intent. The chains can be lifted when we no longer give them power in our lives.

Although the soul is progressing in understanding on its journey through life, there are still pitfalls for the unwary, as shown in Key 16, the Tower. No matter how high we have come or how powerful we think we are, we can be thrown from our tower. Statesmen, movie stars, those who get rich and famous sometimes cannot handle their high positions. Money and power go to their heads, and they and their crowns of glory topple from their high towers. This can happen to the least of us, too. The necessity of balance in all things should never be forgotten.

In Key 17, the Star, the idea of balance is shown clearly as the maiden balances herself between the water of the subconscious and the dry land of the material. The stars are eight-pointed, indicating universal radiant energy.

The moon and the sun have always represented the positive and negative aspects of life. The Moon, Key 18, like the High Priestess, is a guardian of the higher mysteries. Again balance is indicated by the towers of good and evil between which we must pass while we are on the path. A careful study of the Tarot cards and their deep inner meanings and insight can make our journey much smoother, and many pitfalls may be avoided altogether.

The Sun, Key 19, can be thought of as an indication that at last we have mastered the rules of life, the eternal laws, for the sun shines on us as we stay on the positive side of life. The child is our newborn soul which can now ride the horse of passion and energy by his thoughts instead of bridle and bit as before. The red feather in his hair shows that he is one with nature, his nakedness that he no longer has anything to hide.

Key 20, Judgment, the card of spiritual awakening, can be ours when and if we have learned the lessons of the other cards and made them our own. We will then have been born again, will move from death to eternal life. We will be able to live in the world but be not of it, in the sense that most negative, materialistic aspects will no longer affect us.

The ultimate goal is achieved in Key 21, The World, when the self-conscious merges at last with both the subconscious and the super-conscious. Here is humanity as it is meant to be, master of all worlds and dancing lightly while still being a co-creator with the Source. Though the figure on the card is obviously a female, this figure is probably androgenous, having the aspects of both male and female. No longer pairs of opposites, but man in his God aspect of Oneness. The divine Self has at last attained its goal and so he or she can indeed dance through life with complete control of all its aspects— air, fire, water, and earth. This is the ultimate goal for every one of us.

The most important use of the Tarot is to make you think.

When reading the cards for yourself or another, first study the situation and character, also the personality of the person for whom you are reading. The cards may be read on a low level of mere fortune telling, but that is not what they were meant to be used for. Try to judge the seeker, and always give him the most spiritual and philosophical thoughts you can discern in the layout. Perhaps he will understand and even at a later date think back to the pertinent advice the cards have given him for living a successful and happy life.

7.

DIVINATION OF PAST LIVES

This method seems eminently reliable for investigating past lives. I have used it with a number of friends and most of them have felt that in a previous incarnation they were indeed in such a situation as the cards described.

As in the Ancient Celtic Method, pick a Court card to represent the subject of the reading. Place this card in the center of the table. Shuffle the cards well and give them to the seeker. Ask him or her to shuffle the cards with the question in mind, in essence, shuffling the question into the cards. Have the seeker cut the cards into three piles to the left. Pick them up with your left hand. Now you are ready to lay them out.

1. Draw the first card and place it crossways on top of the Court card. This card indicates the conditions under which the seeker lived in a previous life.

2. The next four cards are to be laid out in a square around the seeker's card. Start below with card #2, place card #3 to the left, card #4 above, and card #5 to the right (see Diagram III).

3. Card #3 represents the most important occurrence in the seeker's past life.

4. Card #4, reveals the person who had the most influence over the seeker, either for good or for evil.

5. Card #5 describes the lessons the seeker learned in the past life.

As with other readings, you will try to make a story out of the cards. Perhaps a court card will be at the #2

241

spot instead of #4, but you can still understand the influence and importance of the cards.

One man I read for had a number of pentacles come up, signifying to me that in a past life he was very involved in money. But he said that he felt that the cards indicated a present situation in his life very clearly. It is possible that he had been involved with money and wealth in a previous life. If he did not learn from the experience, he may have had to live it all over again. As we have all probably had many past lives, it would seem that the subconscious would pick out the one for a Tarot reading which would be most helpful and meaning-ful to the seeker at the present time.

DIAGRAM III
THE REINCARNATION METHOD

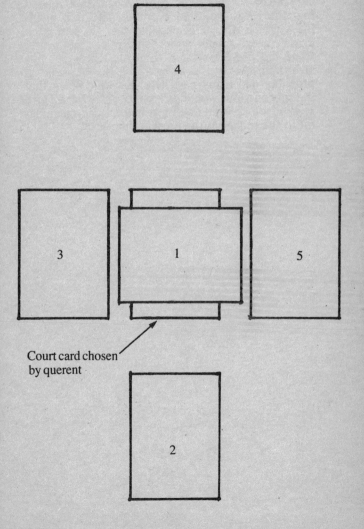

Court card chosen
by querent

GLOSSARY OF SYMBOLS

ANGEL 1. Raphael, angel of air. Symbol of the superconscious (Key #6).

2. Michael, angel of fire and sun (Key #14).

3. Gabriel, angel of water (Key #20).

ANKH Egyptian symbol of life, generation; combines the masculine and feminine (Key #4).

ANUBIS Jackal-headed Egyptian god, representing the evolution of consciousness from lower to to higher levels. He is also the Egyptian equivalent of Hermes or Mercury—signifying self-consciousness, intellectuality (Key #10).

BANNER Also Standard or Flag. Betokens freedom from material bonds, action, vibration. Carried in the left hand, it indicates that control of vibrations has passed from the right hand (self-consciousness) to the left (the subconscious), and has become automatic (Keys #13, 19, 20).

CROSS Solar cross has equal arms to indicate the union of the male, positive element (upright) with female, negative element (horizontal), or the union of God and earth (Keys #2, 20).

CROWN Attainment, mastery. The will, which may be set against the cosmic purpose. Represents the creative, formative and material word Keys #2, 3, 5, 11, 14, 16).

CUBE Sometimes a Square. Represents earth, material manifestation. Order and measurement. That which was, is, and shall be (Key #15).

CUPS Associated with the concept of water (see Suit of Cups, Minor Arcana). The cup is a symbol of knowledge and preservation. It also means love, pleasure and enjoyment (Key #14).

DEVIL Symbolizes the false conception that man is bound by material conditions; that he is a slave to necessity and blind chance. The Devil is sensation divorced from understanding by ignorance (Key #15).

DOG Friend, helper and companion to man. Indicates that all nonhuman forms of life are elevated and improved by the advance of human consciousness (Keys #0, 18).

EAGLE One of the symbols denoting the four seasons, or the four suits of the Minor Arcana. The Eagle is associated with Scorpio (the Scorpion), the 8th sign of the Zodiac. It is a symbol of power (Keys #10, 21).

EARTH Symbol of concrete physical manifestation (Keys #14, 17).

ELLIPSE The superconscious (Key #21).

FIGURE EIGHT ON ITS SIDE Eternal life, the cosmic lemniscate. Harmonious interaction between the conscious and the subconscious, between life and feeling, desire and emotion. May mean dominion over the material (Keys #1, 8).

GLOBE (See Orb of the World.) Symbol of dominion (Key #4).

HEART Symbols in the shape of a heart refer to the subconscious, the emotions (Key #3).

HORSE Symbol of solar energy, or the controlled, subdued life force (Keys #13, 19).

I H V H The ancient Hebrew initials of the name JEHOVAH: I-Fire; H-Water; V-Air; H-Earth (Key #10).

KEYS CROSSED The Hidden Doctrine. One is of silver, the other gold—representing the solar and lunar currents of radiant energy (Key #5).

LIGHTNING A masculine or positive symbol. Lightning flash—the symbol of the life-power that can break down existing forms; a flash of inspiration (Key #16).

LILY Abstract thought, untinged by desire (Key #1).

LION King of the beasts; Zodiacal sign LEO. Represents all powerful subhuman forces. May also stand for Mars (war) (Keys #8, 10, 21).

MIRROR OF VENUS A solar cross surmounted by a circle; symbol of the planet Venus; indicates fertility (Key #3).

MOON A feminine astrological symbol of personality, also of the subconscious mind. The reflected light of the subconscious (Keys #2, 18).

MOUNTAINS (Snow-capped Peaks.) Indicate the cold, abstract principles of mathematics behind and above all warm, colorful and vital activities of cosmic manifestation. Heights of abstract thought. Wisdom and understanding (Keys #0, 4, 9, 14, 20).

ORB OF THE WORLD   A traditional symbol of the earth dominated by the Lord or the Spirit (Key #4).

PALM   Symbol of victory over death, and of the male aspect of life. The active force, as shown on the veil behind the HIGH PRIESTESS (Key #2).

PATH   The way to spiritual attainment and esoteric knowledge, as set forth in the Tarot cards (Keys #14, 18).

PENTACLE   The pentagram in the form of an amulet—believed to protect against evil spirits. (See Suit of Pentacles, also Key #15).

PENTAGRAM   (SEAL OF SOLOMON.) Five-pointed star, expressing mind's domination over the elements. Symbol of the Word made Flesh. Depending on the direction of its points, it may represent order or confusion. Note that the pentagrams are right side up in the Suit of Pentacles, reversed in Key #15.

PILLAR   1. White Pillar (Jachin) establishes the principle inherent in all things, the positive aspect of life; light.
2. Black Pillar (Boaz). Negation of activity, inertia; darkness (Keys #2, 5, 11).

POMEGRANATES   Symbol of the female, passive aspect of life; fecundity (Key #2).

RAM'S HEAD   Symbol of Mars, war; power, leadership. Also First Sign of Zodiac (Aries, the Ram) (Key #4).

ROSE   1. White Rose. Freedom from lower forms of desire and passion.

2. Red Rose. Represents Venus, nature, desire. Both are cultivated flowers, representing cultural activities (Keys #0, 1, 8).

SCALES   Balanced judgment (Key #11).

SCROLL   The Divine Law, the Hidden Mysteries. Past events impressed upon the subsconscious Key #2).

SERPENT   Symbol of wisdom, for it tempts man to knowledge of himself. Secrecy, subtlety. Serpent biting tail represents law of endless transformation; also represents radiant energy descending into manifestation (Keys #1, 6, 10).

SHELLFISH   The early stages of conscious unfoldment. Related to the Zodiacal sign of THE CRAB. May invade the territory of the waking consciousness and give rise to fears (Key #18).

SPHINX   Symbol of the combination of human and animal attributes. The white sphinx betokens mercy; the black one, severity. Sometimes the Sphinx represents the human senses, which are continually propounding riddles (Keys #7, 10).

STAR   Suggests 6th sign of The Zodiac. The 6-point star (hexagram) indicates dominion over laws of the great world; 8-point star represents cosmic order, radiant energy (Keys #9, 17).

STREAM   Symbolizes the stuff of life forever flowing to the ocean of cosmic consciousness (Key #14).

SUN   Source of light, dynamo of radiant energy, whence all creatures derive their personal force (Keys #0, 6, 13, 19).

SUNFLOWERS   Nature in its fullness (Key #19).

SWORDS   Represent activity—either destructive or constructive (see Suit or Swords). They also represent the rigors of the law; can mean the elimination of outworn forms (Key #11).

TOWER   Represents a man's creation or personality, sometimes built on a foundation of false science. Misapprehension; the fallacy of personal isolation (Keys #13, 16, 18).

TREE   1. Tree of Knowledge of Good and Evil, bearing 5 fruits, representing the 5 senses (in Key #6, behind Eve).

2. Tree of Life, bearing 12 fruits, representing the 12 signs of the Zodiac (Key #6, behind Adam).

Note: Under the appellations of the Tree of Life and the Tree of the Knowledge of Good and Evil is concealed the great arcanum of antiquity—the mystery of equilibrium. The Tree of Life represents the spiritual point of balance—the secret of immortality. The Tree of the Knowledge of Good and Evil represents polarity, or unbalance—the secret of mortality. Though humanity is still wandering in the world of good and evil, it will ultimately attain completion and eat of the fruit of the Tree of Life, growing in the midst of the illusionary garden of worldly things.

VEIL   Indicates hidden things or ideas. Symbol of Virginity. Only when veil is rent or penetrated by concentrated impulses on self-conscious levels, are the creative activities of the subconscious realized and actualized (Keys #2, 11).

WAND   Symbol of will and power. Suggests continual renewal of life. May have phallic significance. (See Suit of Wands, also Key #21).

WATER   (Stream, Brook, River, Pool.) Symbolizes the subconscious, the emotions. Water in a pool symbolizes the reservoir of cosmic mind stuff, which can be stirred into vibration by the act of meditation (Keys #14, 17, 18, 20).

WHEEL Symbol of the whole cycle of cosmic expression. The center or pivot is the archetypal or thought world; the inner circle, creative; middle circle, formative; and the outer circle, the material world. The 8 spokes, like the 8-pointed star, represent the channels of universal radiant energy (Keys #7, 10).

WOLF Symbolizes the manifestations of nature before man has tamed and civilized them (Key #18).

WREATH Represents the forces of nature, the kingdom of growing things (Keys #3, 8, 21).

YOD (DROPS OF LIGHT) Yod is the Hebrew letter symbolizing the hands of man. It betokens power, skill, dexterity. The descent of the life-force from above into the conditions of material existence. Corresponds to the Zodiacal sign of the Virgin (Keys #16, 18).

ZERO Symbol of the absence of quality, quantity and mass. Denotes absolute freedom from every limitation. Sign of the infinite and eternal conscious energy. Superconsciousness (Key #0).